# Praise from *Investor's Business Daily* Readers

You have helped take me from a net worth of $697 to over $1 million—honest—since I began reading your paper in 1995.

—J. Moyers

In learning Mr. O'Neil's CAN SLIM method, my husband and I have been able to retire early and build the house of our dreams, and look forward to years of travel in Europe.

—M. Ellis

In just four and a half years, I went from $2,000 to $600,000 (pretax) in my portfolio by going to Bill's seminars and workshops a few times and reading *How To Make Money In Stocks*.

—J. Barkasy

Since I started using CAN SLIM and IBD, and now investors.com, I was able to make 359% on my original investment! IBD has so many features that help me find the great stocks. I'm grateful for all the work you do to help investors.

—K.P.

I place IBD in the same category as my top ranking wealth creation stocks. It's a very important part of my financial assets.

—E. Rivers

My wife and I both retired early because we did not lose as much as most folks did. Thank you, IBD. You are our success.

—S. Gardels

## Praise from Financial Experts

*Investor's Business Daily and the Making of Millionaires* provides an insightful, behind-the-scenes look at how IBD and its founder,

Bill O'Neil, became the successes they are today. For anyone who wants to get into investing, reading this book is a necessary first step.
—David Chalupnik, head of equities,
U.S. Bancorp Asset Management

David Saito-Chung takes an abstract topic, an elaborate investment strategy, and turns it into something understandable and actually enjoyable to read.
—Robert Maltbie, president,
Millennium Asset Management

I always say that "There's always a bull market somewhere," but you will never find it unless you read and understand the way IBD works. This book explains why better than I ever imagined a text could.
—Jim J. Cramer, host,
*Real Money*, a nationally syndicated radio show

*Investor's Business Daily and the Making of Millionaires* carefully chronicles the early years and the myriad of obstacles that the paper had to overcome to reach its current status as one of the "must reads" of the financial press.
—Russ Koesterich,
Chief North American Equity Strategist,
State Street Global Markets

David Saito-Chung has done a masterful job in telling the story of a visionary Wall Street leader, his entrepreneurial philosophy and his fast-growing newspaper.
—Edward Wedbush,
president and chief executive officer,
Wedbush Morgan Securities, Los Angeles

The IBD story is an inspiration for business owners. It reminds us that we continue to learn from our mistakes and that we should develop our ability to correct those mistakes and reach up for new and challenging goals.

—Rob Wilson, president,
Employco Group

As a successful entrepreneur and author, I use *Investor's Business Daily* every day for its information and keen insights on public companies and the markets. David Saito-Chung has written a masterful biography in chronicling how Bill O'Neil started the newspaper and how he prevailed against all naysayers. It is an inspirational story.

—David Silver, president,
Silver Public Relations

This book is a captivating chronicle of the rise of a publication that has emerged as a breath of fresh air for the financial community.

—Sandy Lincoln, president and CEO,
Wayne Hummer Asset Management

This book offers an insightful view on what can truly happen when integrity meets intelligence.

—Glenn Eden,
Weber Shandwick Worldwide

Books by
William J. O'Neil, Founder and Chairman
of *Investor's Business Daily*


*Sports Leaders & Success:*
*55 Top Sports Leaders & How They Achieved Greatness*

*The Successful Investor:*
*What 80 Million People Need to Know to Invest*
*Profitably and Avoid Big Losses*

*How to Make Money in Stocks:*
*A Winning System in Good Times or Bad*

*Business Leaders & Success:*
*55 Top Business Leaders & How They Achieved Greatness*

*24 Essential Lessons for Investment Success:*
*Learn the Most Important Investment Techniques*
*from the Founder of* Investor's Business Daily

# *Investor's Business Daily* and the Making of Millionaires

## How *IBD* Rewrote the Rules of Investing and Business News

### David Saito-Chung

McGraw-Hill

New York   Chicago   San Francisco
Lisbon   London   Madrid   Mexico City   Milan
New Delhi   San Juan   Seoul   Singapore
Sydney   Toronto

3  4  5  6  7  8  9  0    DOC/DOC    0  9  8  7  6  5  4

0-07-145016-5

This publication is designed to provide accurate and authoritative information in regard to the subject matter covered. If legal advice or other expert assistance is required, the services of a competent professional person should be sought.

—From a Declaration of Principles jointly adopted
by a Committee of the American Bar
Association and a Committee of Publishers

McGraw-Hill books are available at special quantity discounts to use as premiums and sales promotions, or for use in corporate training programs. For more information, please write to the Director of Special Sales, Professional Publishing, McGraw-Hill, Two Penn Plaza, New York, NY 10121-2298. Or contact your local bookstore.

 This book is printed on recycled, acid-free paper containing a minimum of 50% recycled de-inked fiber.

# Contents

# Introduction

Never before in history has any one organization like Investor's Business Daily and its affiliates really believed in seriously "helping" human beings really learn the stock market without a "hidden agenda." I sincerely believe in your methods and seriously conclude you like to help people.

Stocks like Franklin Resources, Cisco Systems, Amgen, ATI Medical, Oracle, E-Tek Dynamics, Ascend Communications, NVR Corp., Hovnanian Enterprises, TASER, Urban Outfitters, and others too numerous to mention have made me and my family members a lot of money.

—Lance Preiser, IBD reader

At 11:30 a.m. on April 20, 2004, the *Investor's Business Daily* lunchroom in Los Angeles was buzzing with energy. Some people nibbled on chocolate cake served on blue paper plates with matching napkins. Others sat on white chairs at light blue tables and ate moist carrot cake. Now, there's nothing unusual about eating cake at work. *But at 11:30 in the morning?*

Was this some sit-down strike against the nation's urge to cut carbs? No. After its launch on April 9, 1984, IBD had reached its 20th birthday. But on this day, the newspaper staff celebrated for a different reason.

After two decades of toil and triumphs, of blunders and successes, IBD—not as a newspaper but as an entrepreneurial start-up—was finally having its cake and eating it too.

"I'm happy to announce that IBD turned a profit in the month of March," Bill O'Neil told a cheering crowd of about 100 people that day inside the bright, glassy room. "They said it couldn't be done. But we did it!"

O'Neil, the founder and chairman of America's youngest national newspaper, said the paper had cut costs, increased efficiency and opened up new channels of revenue. Having met his profit goal in March, O'Neil said he was setting a new goal of making the paper achieve 30% pretax profit margins in the future. He pledged a new quarterly bonus plan for IBD associates. He also urged the staff to work more closely with people in different departments. After the five-minute talk, people hung around and chatted for a little longer. Then it was back to work.

The paradox about IBD is this: It's helped the paper's readers make a lot of money in the market, but the newspaper itself lost money for a long time. Of course, that's typical in the newspaper industry.

"I did expect it would be profitable in five or six years," O'Neil said in an interview. "I feel we didn't do enough research to understand the complexities of the newspaper business. It was probably good we didn't. Otherwise, we might not have started it."

Running a newspaper is expensive. From USA Today's launch in September 1982 through the first half of 1987, the cutting-edge daily lost about $233 million. It scored its first year of profit in 1993. Chapter 3 in this book, "Lessons for All Entrepreneurs," offers glimpses of the problems IBD faced on the road to profitability and the changes the paper made to turn things around.

## The Message Is Important

For O'Neil, profitability isn't the only thing that's meaningful and important.

Helping readers understand how the stock market truly works has value, even if this accomplishment doesn't get quantified in the income statement. This has been IBD's mission from the start. The U.S. stock market lost an estimated $7 trillion in shareholder wealth during the 2000–02 bear market. During that dark period, rays of light touched IBD's doorstep in the form of readers' testimonials. These readers sent letters or gave taped interviews at IBD seminars saying they had listened to IBD's analysis of the market top in 2000, went into cash and saved their portfolios from a lot of pain. Many IBD readers saved millions of dollars.

For a financial newspaper, there's perhaps nothing more gratifying than that.

How could a newspaper achieve this? Well, IBD isn't a conventional newspaper.

There aren't any sports pages, no weather forecasts, no horoscope, no person-to-person classifieds, no personal advice syndicated columns. You won't find a review of the latest musical on Broadway. IBD, at its heart, is a daily education on sound stock investing based on 50 years of fact-based stock market research. It is a unique tool and information source that helps investors build wealth through buying, holding and eventually selling the best growth stocks in the market. Along the way, the paper has debunked many myths on investing (including "buy on the dips," "avoid stocks with high P-E ratios" and "diversify your holdings") by highlighting the most relevant data for finding these big winners.

IBD's associates are passionate about helping readers achieve success. One vice president proposed the idea of a book to O'Neil in the aftermath of the 2000–02 bear market, a plunge that years from now will be compared with the Dutch tulip bulb craze of the late

1500s to early 1600s. She urged O'Neil and her colleagues to help the millions of investors out there who watched the tech bubble pop in 2000 and then sat on the sidelines helplessly as the bear market crushed their portfolios. "If every investor had the sell rules IBD teaches, can you imagine how much damage would have been avoided?" she said.

O'Neil responded by writing *The Successful Investor*, published in August 2003. This book is also a product of that associate's conviction.

Adhering to the IBD sell rules would have enabled every investor who owned stock directly to side-step the carnage without knowing a thing about the market. How? All an investor had to do was follow IBD's golden rule: Sell and cut losses if your stock falls 7% or 8% below your purchase price. True, it's easy to say and hard to do. It's also true that in the market you can often be your own worst enemy. Investing without some form of discipline is like driving a sports car without a seat belt. NASCAR drivers wear one. In the stock arena, a set of sound sell rules is that seat belt. You can get a taste of these rules by reading the second half of Chapter 2.

IBD has also helped illuminate the truth about the enduring strength of the U.S. economy. A free-enterprise system, lower taxes, good old American ingenuity, optimism and perseverance have all helped the U.S. earn and keep its badge as the world's richest economy. The proof is in the paper. Over the years, it's told tons of stories about the amazing growth of this country. In 1984, the paper had 18 pages. Now, it has two sections of usually 14 or 16 pages each. The IBD weekly special edition on Mondays is often 40 pages strong. Chapter 4 outlines many of the things IBD has found that are good about the economy.

In every interview he's had with other media outlets, O'Neil has always refused to say how much the paper has lost or how much its expenses have been each year. Since IBD is part of Data Analysis, Incorporated, the holding company for all of O'Neil's companies including IBD, O'Neil doesn't have to disclose such figures anyway. He didn't give any data to this reporter either. So one can only imagine how happy he was to announce the good news of IBD's March 2004 profits. Years ago, the paper made money for three or four months by slashing marketing expenses, O'Neil says. That didn't last because IBD continued to face heavy ad and delivery costs as it sought to expand circulation.

Some have sensed that in recent years, O'Neil has sharply changed his way of thinking about IBD. For years, he thought that it was okay for the paper to lose money because it could be funded by his profitable enterprises. The paper's mission—to help investors learn how the market really works—appeared to be priority number 1. O'Neil's thinking has changed. In 2000, O'Neil hired one of the world's top management consulting firms and asked them to study the paper's circulation and marketing efforts. Problem was, he wouldn't let them see all the data. In 2003, O'Neil invited management consultants again, only this time he asked a Boston Consulting Group team and IBD management to work together and focus on one goal: Make the paper profitable. Do whatever it takes. By this time all assumptions that a hefty circulation would bring a wellspring of advertising and hoist the paper into the black were for the most part gone.

IBD is much more than a paper now.

It now has a PDF- and Web-based version called *e*IBD™ the Investor's Business Daily® Digital Edition. Its Web site www.investors.com supplies a wide range of proprietary screens and information to help investors find great stocks. It's teamed up with Daily Graphs® investment research tool, a William O'Neil + Co., Incorporated, product that is one of the most sophisticated stock-screening tools in the U.S. for serious investors who aren't pro money managers. IBD is also a series of hands-on workshops across the country helping investors learn how to pick the best stocks, buy and sell correctly, and manage their portfolios with success.

"IBD is a multimedia powerhouse with unique information that no one has been able to duplicate," noted Kathy Sherman, IBD's head of communications.

IBD now enjoys income from multiple revenue streams. And like the millions of young Japanese who turn 20 and join a "Coming of Age" ceremony on Jan. 15 every year, IBD reached its own coming of age in 2004. It's living its own American dream. It's become profitable.

## What's His Name?

Practically every American investor knows Warren Buffett. Market pros and the press unanimously hail him as the king of value investors. Yet the media has never really gotten down to deciding on a king of *growth* investors. If it did, Bill O'Neil would perhaps show up among the top choices.

So why don't many people know O'Neil? Why is he, as one employee says, an enigma?

You can get to know more about him by reading a profile in Chapter 5, "Not All News Should Be Bad News." But for starters, O'Neil and Buffett are in some ways like night and day. Buffett heads a public company, Berkshire Hathaway. Public companies must file quarterly and annual reports about everything—from earnings and sales to whether they're suing or being sued, to all the financial and business risks they face—with the Securities and Exchange Commission. Most public firms send news releases to every major news agency in the country. O'Neil heads a group of private firms. Private companies don't have to disclose as much to the public. That's why you'll probably never see the CEO of Mars, Inc., the privately owned maker of M&M's chocolate candies, on CNBC.

Buffett is synonymous with the successful investments he's made and described for his readers in the *Washington Post:* Coca-

Cola, See's Candies and Geico Insurance. Buffett has graced magazine covers. Many people have written books about him. In 1997, Wiley published Janet Lowe's compilation of his quips and quotes in *Warren Buffett Speaks: Wit and Wisdom from the World's Greatest Investor*. Phil Schroeder composed a CD of music called "Oracle of Omaha Soundtrack" that injects snippets of Buffett talking—yes, just talking!—into contemporary folk songs of guitar and banjo. O'Neil, in contrast, has written a lot of books—not about himself but about how to pick a great growth stock and how to avoid devastating losses in the market. Sure, IBD readers who attend the paper's highest-level seminar ask for his autograph. Yet the national glossies aren't exactly rushing to get him on next week's cover.

O'Neil perhaps isn't interested in getting publicity for himself personally. When someone tossed onto my desk a grocery bag full of articles written about O'Neil and IBD, I could find only one that had a picture of O'Neil at a party. He prefers to spend the evenings and weekend quietly with his family or close friends.

While some reporters have poked fun at O'Neil's reserved ways, others have picked up on what O'Neil is really like.

> William O'Neil, publisher of *Investor's Daily*, is a quiet man who keeps a low profile. To get him talking, ask him about his data.
>
> "That's where we're outstanding," he said, suddenly animated. "If you're interested in investment [sic] at all you're really crazy not to take this newspaper."
>
> *Investor's Daily*, which made its debut in April, hopes to take on the *Wall Street Journal* as the paper the financial community consults with its morning coffee. Headquartered in Los Angeles, it is printed on both coasts and moving gradually toward national distribution.

"My emphasis is to get quality items of news and statistics nobody has ever seen before," O'Neil said.

— Gail Collins, United Press
International, October 1984

In a 1987 article, Chris Barnett also painted a realistic portrait of O'Neil the man and what it takes to do well in the market:

O'Neil, at 54, is a bit of a mystery man. He's a populist Demo-crat who plugs Reagan and his policies. He's quiet, single-mindedly shrewd, and sits in a darkened office lit only by three computer screens and a Big Board digital ticker that gallops across the wall. He is also a master at explaining—in plain English and a soft Texas drawl—how investors can get rich and how they can lose. Spend a couple hours with him and he makes it all seem so easy. Yet therein lies the danger. O'Neil does his homework. Most people don't.

## Humble as Pie

As *USA Today* jumped past the *Wall Street Journal* to become the country's most read newspaper, its founder, Al Neuharth, celebrated with abandon. He held a party inside his vast office, complete with a panoramic view of Washington, D.C., and a spiral staircase to the 31st floor. Inside was a white-onyx fireplace big enough, the *Washington Post* wrote, "to roast a steer." Neuharth had a larger-than-life bust sculpture of himself placed in the newspaper building's lobby in Arling-ton, Va. *USA Today* cartoonist David Seavey commented that the bust was so big it belonged on a mountain, Peter Prichard wrote in "The Making of McPaper: The Inside Story of USA Today." Neuharth had two more statues made: One was placed outside his corporate head-quarters office, and the other at a printing plant in Brevard County, Fla.

O'Neil, in contrast, seems to live by the old Japanese saying: "A wise hawk hides its claws" (*No-aru taka wa tsume-wo kakusu*). His old Toyota has a tiny crack in the windshield. His office at IBD runs 24 feet long by 11 feet wide. The plain white walls and gray carpet are the same color as the ad sales office next door and the newsroom. Despite the ocean being a mere 2 miles away, O'Neil's office windows face the employee parking lot and the 90 freeway, perhaps the shortest federal freeway in the U.S. Just a few hundred yards further is La Ballona Creek, a canal encased in concrete that originates in downtown LA and snakes for miles through the city's sprawl before it feeds into the Pacific. O'Neil's metal desk is big, but not huge. He keeps an eye on the market with two large desktop computer screens. In earlier days, his office wall had a real-time electronic ticker tape running during the whole trading day.

O'Neil is all about honesty. A Dec. 21, 1987, *BusinessWeek* article (page 121) on O'Neil opened with a story that one day he came into a meeting with two bodyguards at his side and one million dollars' worth of cash in a briefcase. He walked into a meeting with his sales staff, emptied the cash onto the table, and told them if they worked hard they could become rich! Then he put all the money back into the briefcase and had it taken back to the bank. Years later, O'Neil dismisses the story as half-true: "I had only one bodyguard, and there wasn't a million dollars in that briefcase!"

His strong belief in the principles of truth and honesty has frequently paid off. His stock research and brokerage firm, William O'Neil + Co., was awarded the first contract in the U.S. to manage money for the Vatican, O'Neil says. Sometime in the late 1960s, the Instituto per le Opere di Religione, the official bank of the Vatican, gave O'Neil's firm a $25 million stock portfolio to supervise and manage. O'Neil managed the account for a year or two. Then one day, the Instituto suggested to O'Neil that it would appear better for them if the business was processed through an investment management company based in Rome rather than one based in the U.S. "The logic presented to us sounded fine, and we agreed to process it through their sources based on the suggestions made by the Vatican and the Vatican Bank," O'Neil said.

Then one day, O'Neil was asked to pay for a secretary and other business expenses at the investment firm. He was also offered the opportunity to become a part owner with a one-third ownership. O'Neil turned it down because he didn't really know the people at the investment management firm in Rome. Plus, the idea of having to pay expenses "just didn't smell right." He sent a letter to the Instituto stating, "We hereby resign the account" and sent a check of roughly $31 million. It was a big piece of O'Neil's business in the early 1970s.

Things broke open afterward. In March 1980, Michele Sindona, head of the Rome money management firm, was convicted in the U.S. of fraud and perjury in the 1974 collapse of the New York–based Franklin National Bank. He went to jail. Sindona's protégé Roberto Calvi, who headed the failed Milan-based Banco Ambrosiano, was found hanged under Blackfriar's Bridge in London in June 1982. Later, the U.S. media reported that Italian prosecutors charged U.S.–born Archbishop Paul Marcinkus, who headed the Vatican Bank, and two bank officials "with accessories to fraudulent bankruptcy" in the collapse of Banco Ambrosiano.

Someone once asked me what the most important thing was that eventually allowed me to achieve my rather limited success. My parents were divorced when I was 1 year old—those were Depression years, and we were just emerging from them. My grandmother was the leader of the clan. We all lived together with my aunt, uncle and mother. Grandmother was religious, insisted on my going to church, and although I didn't always like that as a kid, as I look back on it, it was THE single most important thing, because I learned the difference between right and wrong. It's been very valuable at several junctures in the business world because there's always some-one coming to you saying, "I'll do this if you'll do that." And it's usually something that isn't of the best from an ethical point of view. So I've been able to steer clear of major prob-lems because I just don't participate unless something seems to be right and makes good sense.

—William O'Neil

Like Buffett, Bill O'Neil has hit many home runs in the stock mar-ket. He's created a new type of investor: one who understands how the market really works and can make smart, independent decisions on growth stocks based on relevant and reliable data. IBD is O'Neil's way of sharing his knowledge and techniques with as many people as he can. It is an enduring legacy to investors that has made millionaires and dramatically changed lives.

Truly, IBD is a slice of O'Neil himself: data driven, passionate about success, starved for the truth, positive not negative, seeking to empower investors and continually looking for new opportunities to join in the growth and future prosperity of America.

## About This Book

Whether you're a veteran user of www.investors.com, an investor who's never picked up a copy of IBD, a member of the media or a book reviewer or critic, please view this book as only a slice of IBD. This book is based on a half dozen interviews with O'Neil and short interviews with a number of IBD's management. I was not presented a view into the paper's financials. Still, my intention at all times was not to produce a puff piece. As you'll find in Chapters 1 and 3, I've tried my best to paint a realistic portrait of the newspaper, warts included.

As an employee of IBD, I did write this book with one strong bias—that the system of rules on how to select, buy and sell growth stocks really does work for anyone who puts in the recommended time and effort and is willing to accept the fact that he or she will make mistakes. Like every other investor, I've taken my lumps as I've been learning about bull and bear markets, about charts, and about stocks when they get hot and when they get cold. And I've learned a lot about myself in the process.

In a strong bull market like the one we saw in 2003, IBD can help dedicated readers who follow all the rules—let me repeat, ALL the rules!—smash the market's return.

# CHAPTER 1

# Naysayers and Nervous Rivals

This telephone has too many short-comings to be seriously considered as a means of communication.
>—Western Union internal memo, 1876

Everything that can be invented, has been invented.
>—Charles Duell, commissioner of the
>U.S. Office of Patents, 1899

Airplanes are interesting toys but of no military value.
>—Marechal Ferdinand Foch (1851–1929),
>professor of strategy,
>Ecole supérieure de guerre military school, Paris

Who the hell wants to hear actors talk?
>—H. M. Warner, Warner Bros., 1927

There is no reason anyone would want a computer in their home.
>—Ken Olsen, founder, Digital Equipment Corp., 1977

We don't feel there is a huge market for that kind of material. We think the words do a better job.

—Lawrence Armour, *Wall Street Journal* spokesman,
on IBD's plan to put more data in stock tables
to help investors pick superior growth stocks,
as quoted by Thomas Rosenstiel, "New Financial
Newspaper to Start," *Los Angeles Times*, April 5, 1984

Sure. Uh huh. Anything you say.

Human resistance to change certainly hasn't changed.

Whenever someone challenges the establishment with an innovative product or a bold new idea, he or she must often cross a river awash with three "isms": criticism, pessimism and skepticism. William O'Neil, who started IBD after becoming convinced the public needed better information to make smarter decisions on stocks, found he was no exception.

In November 1983, O'Neil laid out his plans to start *Investor's Daily* (the original name of the paper until Sept. 16, 1991), a brand-new national business paper. It would differ from the *Wall Street Journal*, the industry's heavyweight champ for the past 100 years, in several ways. IBD would give, on a daily basis, special ratings for every stock in its tables to measure profit growth and stock-price strength: the Earnings Per Share (EPS) Rating and the Relative Price Strength (RS) Rating (please see the glossary for details on these two proprietary ratings).

This was revolutionary. Why? Investors across America would be able to compare stocks against all other stocks for the first time ever.

That wasn't all. The paper would print large charts of the major indexes so readers could study the market's overall price trend. IBD would also run about 100 small weekly charts that would catch stocks rocketing to or trading near their 52-week highs. Why? Every stock that makes a big run must at some point hit a 52-week high or an all-time high. This daily screen would thus ensure that no great stock would be passed up or ignored. IBD would also feature a growing company in extraordinary detail. And it would update a table of nearly 200 different industry groups ranked in terms of six-month relative price performance. This would show which sectors were the leaders of the market and which ones were the duds.

That wasn't all. IBD wouldn't list the price-to-earnings ratio or dividends in its tables, at least at the start. Why? Because O'Neil found in his study of the greatest growth stocks in the 1950s, 1960s and 1970s that both were mostly useless in figuring out a stock's growth potential. Rather, outstanding earnings and sales growth and long-lasting demand for shares from institutional investors proved to be much more important factors. IBD also wouldn't give buy or sell recommendations for any stock. In short, IBD wouldn't be like any other financial daily, weekly or monthly.

Many thought IBD would suffer an early death.

"I wouldn't give it a year," the *New York Times* quoted William Garrison, head of the investment advisory firm Garrison, Keogh & Co., as saying. According to the June 27, 1984, article, he "and others felt that the potential audience for such a data-crammed publication is too small to find sufficient circulation and advertising" (Business Section, page 1).

"Let's just say it's not going to put the *Wall Street Journal* out of business," a stockbroker at Paine Webber Mitchell chimed, according to a San Francisco–area business journal in March 1984. Perhaps the most colorful comment came from Gordon Crawford. In a Nov. 21, 1983, *Ad Week* piece, the Capitol Research analyst said, "When you look at the entrenched positions of the *Wall Street Journal* and other regular business media, what O'Neil wants to do is like trying to scale Mount Everest in your skivvies" (page 8).

Some of IBD's potential competitors, however, showed a little respect. After O'Neil announced in late 1983 that he was going to start a new financial publication, *Forbes* editor Jim Michaels flew to Los Angeles to meet O'Neil. At the time, it wasn't clear whether O'Neil was planning to sell a newspaper or a magazine. So the No. 2 man at *Forbes* told O'Neil, "I hope you aren't going to start a competing magazine."

A few years later, Michael Bloomberg, the founder of *Bloomberg News*, walked up to O'Neil at a conference and said, "If you'll stay out of my business, I'll stay out of yours." O'Neil just grinned.

On the eve of IBD's thrust into the media universe, O'Neil vowed success. "Anyone in America who comes out with a better product, a higher quality product, will succeed," he said at a news conference in April 1984. In a free country, few would argue with this law of business. Yet folks like Thomas Rosenstiel of the *Los Angeles Times* had trouble believing O'Neil. In an April 5, 1984 piece, Rosenstiel wrote such reasoning "might as easily serve as justification for producing a new cheese-filled chicken frank" (Business Section, page 1).

## Fallen Challengers

IBD wasn't the first to cross swords with the *Journal*. In 1971, Media General Inc. started *Financial Daily*. Like IBD, it had lots of charts and tables. But *Financial Daily*'s circulation peaked at 10,000. In less than 12 months, it threw in the towel and morphed into a weekly.

Perhaps *Financial Daily* suffered from the fact that it made the plunge during what turned out to be one of America's worst economic decades of the 20th century. In 1974, the Nifty Fifty stocks began to rust. The market stumbled into bear territory and hibernated for the next nine years. On Aug. 13, 1979, *BusinessWeek* ran a cover piece— "The Death of Equities"—that would continue to gain fame well beyond its initial publication.

When asked later for his opinion of the prospects for IBD, Media General's vice chairman Alan Donnahue told the *LA Times* in April 1984, "What we found in a nutshell is that there is just not enough daily demand for this kind of information" (page 2). He too seemed to suggest IBD would fail.

IBD fired back. Stephen Fox, the paper's president and a veteran reporter from the Associated Press, argued that IBD would not fail because it was not like the *Financial Daily*. He pointed out that one difference between the two ventures, for example, was that the *Financial Daily* had been priced too high at a buck per copy during its short life on the market. In contrast, IBD was selling its paper at the newsstands for 35 cents a copy. Another difference was the condition of the U.S. economy. In the years that had passed from when the *Financial Daily* had been closed down, the economy had weathered two oil shocks and stagflation. It had gotten back on the growth track, and demand for business and financial information had swollen. Finally, unlike the mid- to late 1970s, IBD was coming aboard in the middle of a baby bull market. The Dow had scored a follow-through rally on Aug. 17, 1982, and that rally grew 68% over the next 16 months. Some observers say that the *Financial Daily* had experienced serious printing problems. Sometimes certain parts of its stock tables were garbled. Sometimes key data were omitted. IBD was sure it could avoid those problems.

To get his newspaper off the ground, O'Neil had studied the best papers in the industry. He had checked out the *Journal* because it had the best profit margins and the highest return on equity at the time. He had analyzed Gannett Co.'s launch of *USA Today*, and he had concluded that the colorful, easy-to-read paper's fortunes depended heavily on its success at the newsstand. O'Neil said IBD would live or die by its subscriptions.

## Not All Were Naysayers

In a June 27, 1984, article titled "Investor's Daily: Fight for Life," the *New York Times* noted some readers liked the "in-depth analysis of one company each day, with voluminous statistical data including the number of shares owned by various mutual funds and a 15-year monthly price history" (page 35).

"The paper is 'something any portfolio manager should look at first thing in the morning,' said A. Michael Kailing, president of A.M. Kailing & Associates Ltd., a Chicago manager of corporate pension funds," the *Times* wrote. It also noted that readers liked the use of "heavy black type" in the tables to flag stocks that had made sharp price increases the previous day. *Times* writer Alex Jones wrote that neither the *Times* nor the *Journal* had this feature.

"It cost Gannett maybe $100 million in the first 15 months of publication [of *USA Today*]," *Advertising Age* quoted Bruce Thorp, an analyst at Lynch, Jones & Ryan, as saying in a Nov. 14, 1983, article. "It's difficult to see how a group like this will do what they say they're going to do." But according to the Los Angeles–based *Daily News*, Thorp also said, "I'm enthused by the lack of puffery. They didn't make all kinds of wild claims. It's a pretty ambitious project, but at the same time it's starting off modestly enough that it might work" (page 2).

O'Neil had smaller startup costs and more capital than would someone who was building a national newspaper from scratch. Among the assets and income he could draw upon were his stock research and charting services for institutional investors—the big boys of the market, including mutual funds, banks, pension funds, university endowments, insurers and hedge funds. Back then, William O'Neil + Co. charged each of its roughly 400 customers anywhere from $50,000 to $500,000 in trading commission fees a year. The company's database also supplied the paper's proprietary stock ratings and screens to identify the premier growth stocks of the market. O'Neil's Daily Graphs® weekly chart books boasted more than 25,000 subscribers, each paying

$200 for an annual subscription. O'Neil also owned a printing factory in Los Angeles that he had started several years before. Today, O'Neil Data Systems, Inc. (ODS), makes online directories and customized publications for large corporations including FedEx, DHL Express, Blue Cross, Visa and Toyota/Lexus.

O'Neil was ready to milk these cash cows to fund the paper's expensive operations.

## From the Goliath's Mouth

The bigwigs at the *Wall Street Journal* made comments that blended graciousness, respect, arrogance and cool indifference.

In an April 23, 1984, column in *New York* magazine, WSJ associate publisher Peter Kann said, "There hasn't been a major discussion here about the paper, and I've only just glanced at it. But we welcome all new publications, and we have no reason to wish this one ill" (page 18).

"It's a very gutsy thing to come into the newspaper business today. We wish him luck," the *Los Angeles Times* quoted *Journal* spokesman Lawrence Armour as saying in Rosenstiel's April 5, 1984, piece (page 1).

"No one's losing any sleep over this," Frederick Taylor, executive editor of the *Journal*, said in an April 6, 1984, *Newsday* article. "When the [*New York*] *Times* started a national edition, we watched that. When *USA Today* started, we watched that. And we'll watch this." Taylor also tipped his hat by adding, "Mr. O'Neil's a smart guy, and he's not to be underrated."

The *Journal's* attitude was no surprise. After all, with nearly 2 million subscribers across the nation, the 100-year-old organization simply dominated its industry. Asked about IBD's strategy to offer beefed-up stock tables and charts, WSJ editors yawned. "We don't feel there is a huge market for that kind of material," Armour said (as quoted by Rosenstiel). "We think the words do a better job."

The very idea of a challenger going head to head with the king of the jungle excited more than a few folks in the industry. O'Neil's brain child attracted a band of about 20 writers, editors and sales staff from the nation's top papers and news organizations. They included the AP, *Barron's*, *BusinessWeek*, *Forbes* and the *San Francisco Examiner*. Maryanne McNellis, a veteran *BusinessWeek* writer and editor, became the paper's first editor. She recruited staff from large dailies in the Southern California area. LaMont Hutchins left Dow Jones to head circulation, while Bill Gallagher, who directed corporate advertising for the *New York Times*, joined as head of IBD's East Coast advertising.

"There were a lot of risk takers in the newsroom," recalled Terry Jones, who was also hired from *BusinessWeek* and has been with the paper from the start. "For me, it was choosing between an established place that was stagnant, like UPI, and a new start-up, a national newspaper taking on the *Wall Street Journal*. It was a once-in-a-lifetime opportunity. What more could you ask for?"

## A Sluggish Start

The first edition of IBD rolled off the presses on April 9, 1984. It cost 35 cents at the newsstand, 15 cents less than what the *Journal* charged. A yearlong subscription cost $84. O'Neil had high hopes. He told the media that he expected circulation to grow to 50,000 within six months. The paper would become profitable within 18 months, or around October 1985.

Looking back, O'Neil's circulation targets seemed fair. At the start, IBD flew, trucked and hand-delivered 30,000 copies in 30 major cities in 11 western states plus New York. O'Neil hoped to sell 50,000 copies a day by the end of the year.

The targets were too optimistic. By the end of 1984, circulation had failed to breach 30,000. It was well below what IBD had been hoping for. Circulation didn't break past 50,000 until the period ended in September 1986, according to the Audit Bureau of Circulations (ABC). The media, citing former employees at IBD, estimated that the paper lost about $10 million a year. O'Neil won't disclose exactly how much IBD has lost over the years.

Other problems popped up. In Northern California's Santa Clara and San Mateo counties, home of Silicon Valley, more than 250 of about 325 IBD newspaper boxes were sabotaged by vandals in the first month IBD went on sale. "Company officials believe one person or group is responsible for the wrecked boxes and they have hired a private investigator to track down the culprit, said LaMont Hutchins, director of circulation," according to a Bay Area business journal in its May 7, 1984, weekly edition (page 6). The attacks on the boxes in towns such as Cupertino, San Jose and Los Gatos weren't happening in any of the 30 other cities where IBD was being sold, Hutchins said.

The financial newspaper industry was rocked by scandal in August 1984. *Wall Street Journal* reporter R. Foster Winans was found guilty of charges that he gave information on which stocks he would write about to his roommates, who subsequently made large profits on the inside information.

Things got hot under the collar at IBD as well. The pace of writing stories was intense. Some reporters had to churn out three stories a week, regardless of the news beat. According to the newspaper trade paper *Bulldog Reporter* in September 1984, some insiders called the newsroom a "byline derby." One writer quit after complaining about having to write only business briefs.

Yet some say most writers didn't really know what exactly O'Neil was looking for. They didn't quite understand how he viewed companies and the economy. Back then, journalists had grown up reading and watching stories about Watergate, not about exactly how companies like Boeing, Houston Oil & Minerals, Limited, Liz Claiborne, Merck and McDonald's were growing profits and sales rapidly. They wanted to be like Bob Woodward and Carl Bernstein, the *Washington Post* reporters who traced a scandal all the way to President Richard Nixon, which ultimately led to Nixon's resignation. They wanted to expose what's bad about business and the government.

O'Neil held an opposite objective. His exhaustive study of the best stocks in past decades had helped him discover what makes America truly great: the entrepreneurial spirit that gives birth to new products and services, which in turn make people's lives richer and provide new jobs for tens or even hundreds of thousands of people. This is the lifeblood of a dynamic economy. The study was original, and O'Neil made a lot of money through his research. So he was more interested in helping investors find out which firms were the most efficiently run, the fastest growing and the best managed. O'Neil fought a thick-as-blood ethos that journalists should find out who's corrupt and give business a good swift kick in the rear once in a while to keep it honest.

"A lot of journalists moaned that they were being forced into some kind of IBD mold. But O'Neil was more patient with his journalists than most leaders would have been," said Jones, who is now economics editor and an editorial writer for IBD. "It's hard to find what's positive, what's growing in the economy. The paper has always been skewed toward growth, just like the U.S. economy has been for the past 100 years."

"I'm surprised that he stuck with it. It would have been easy for O'Neil to write the paper off as a noble experiment gone awry and get rid of it," Jones added. "He could have gone off and done other things that would have made a lot of money. Beyond the newspaper as a business, he had a belief in its mission."

Jones says he got a valuable education in how to dive into a company's financial statements and discover real nuggets of growth. Why? The paper's management made him learn how to analyze other companies the way O'Neil had been doing for more than two decades. For a while, the editors kicked him out of the newsroom. Instead, he reported to Connie Cullen, who worked for O'Neil's institutional research firm, to learn exactly how earnings should be calculated. He learned how to strip out extraordinary items, to compare year-over-year figures, and to study revenue growth as well in order to see whether a company was truly growing. "I eventually got it," he said.

## It Sure Isn't the Brokerage Business

In addition to a circulation of 125,000, O'Neil figured the paper would need roughly nine pages of ads a day to be profitable. In the early years, it didn't come close. After the paper got going, O'Neil soon learned that the newspaper business and the stock research business were about as different as, to borrow from Mark Twain, a lightning bug and lightning.

O'Neil crushed his competitors in terms of the charts he sold to money managers. In fact, it would be an injustice to simply call them "charts." Today, the charts sold by William O'Neil + Co. have as many as 150 different pieces of information about a company, with more than half related to the company's business fundamentals, not its stock-price action. That's why they're called *Datagraphs®*, which is a registered trademark.

The newspaper business, however, was a totally different animal. O'Neil found that the *Wall Street Journal* simply dominated the competition in terms of ad sales. The *Journal* had an iron grip on the advertising purse strings of major companies across the nation. This was bad news for IBD. Experts say up to 70% of revenue from the newspaper business comes from ads.

The *Journal* and other mainstream publications spent decades and lots of dollars building strong relationships with both ad firms and the corporations with big ad budgets. The ties were so close that one could call it an "elite club." The cozy relationships between the *Journal* and the ad firms caught O'Neil off-guard. The *Journal* would host concerts with famous rock bands and invite all the young folks who worked at the ad firms. Then they'd go back and tell everyone at the office what a wonderful time they had had.

Those concerts weren't free lunches. According to a Nov. 17, 1983, article in the *Los Angeles Herald Examiner*, the *Journal* charged $62,852.64 for a full-page ad in all its editions (page 15, section A). In the beginning, IBD asked for $1,000 for a page. That's no ordinary gap. That's the newspaper industry's version of the Grand Canyon. Imagine: You just opened a hamburger shop and charged 10 cents for a quality burger and fries while the shop down the street that's been around for 47 years charged $6.20.

"We were very naïve, and we didn't even really realize it [the newspaper business] was the advertising business. So it took us a year or two to figure that out," O'Neil said in a March 18, 2002, interview with the *Los Angeles Business Journal* (page 26).

The IBD staff soon found that the door into this "club" of big national dailies, big weeklies and the ad agencies was hard to get open. In the early going, only a few companies ran regular ads in the paper: steel products maker Quanex, Charles Schwab (which didn't go public until 1987) and a luxury property developer in the Palm Springs, Calif., area.

## "The IBD Difference"

Although IBD struggled early on in the quest for full-page ads, a glimmer of hope appeared in the form of an IBD news release on Feb. 5, 1985. The paper announced that a survey showed its readers had an average annual income of $123,172, 45% higher than the $84,900 income for the average *Wall Street Journal* reader. The IBD subscriber had a personal investment portfolio of $311,700. Point: Wealthier readers were quickly finding value in IBD. O'Neil said that 25% of those surveyed said they were spending less time with the *Journal*.

IBD began to mine a new market.

"These figures clearly show that we are attracting the type of readers we targeted—high-income individuals with large portfolios and an active interest in business and investments," O'Neil said in a company press release. "It shows we are on track with our game plan . . . and gaining on the *Journal*."

Readers in Florida and other places got their paper *two days after the publication date* because in 1984 IBD was printed in only two places: Los Angeles and New York. Yet from early on, Florida became a hub of IBD subscribers.

> From the beginning, we knew we had something different. When someone missed a copy of their paper (and we missed a lot of deliveries with only a few print sites), they got very upset. Delivery complaints were our big challenge in the early days because readers knew its value—that it gave them more information in picking stocks and validating their ideas. We knew we were helping people make better decisions—not by opinion, but with information based on how the market works.
>
> —Harlan Ratzky, vice president, Internet marketing

In a letter to readers on the paper's one-year anniversary on April 9, 1985, Fox gave more good news. IBD has subscribers in all 50 U.S. states, "even though some can't get the paper on the issue date," Fox wrote on the front page. Three out of 10 subscribers were officers in their organizations. One out of nearly eight readers was a professional money manager. One-third of these readers oversaw $100 million to $1 billion in assets.

"What this survey, along with comments from subscribers, tells us is that we have succeeded in producing a high-quality publication which has attracted a sophisticated audience," Fox wrote. "Many people tell us that *Investor's Daily* has become their 'first read' because it's superior to other business publications. We are very proud of that."

Later surveys confirmed the fact that IBD was carving its own niche in the business and investment news arena. A 1991 study found that IBD subscribers had an average household income of $260,000 and an average net worth of $2.4 million, up $1 million from 1988. What's more, 62% of subscribers who were employed held top-management posts, and 22% owned their own businesses.

## Convincing Doubting Thomases One at a Time

Meanwhile, IBD sales staff met with stockbrokers across the country. "Oh, we already get the *Journal*, we don't need another financial paper," most of them would say. But Kathy Sherman and other sales staff told them IBD wasn't the *Journal* because it was totally different.

> "How so?"
> "We have an Earnings Per Share Rating, which allows you to compare a company to all other companies in terms of their ability to grow profits."
> "Oh yeah? Hey, that is different."

These quick conversations enabled Sherman, who is now IBD vice president for communications, to get these places to lower the drawbridge. Slowly, people began to realize that IBD was not some copycat of another publication. It gave something new and revolutionary.

Sherman found that top money managers picked up on the uniqueness of the paper fast.

She once knocked on the doors of Capital Research, a big-time money management firm in Los Angeles to which William O'Neil +

Co. had been trying to sell its research. She met with a roomful of executives and gave her pitch. At the end of the meeting, they all smiled and shook her hand. Many took subscriptions on the spot. When Sherman later told O'Neil about the meeting and relayed some of Capital Research's questions she couldn't answer, he jumped out of his chair. "You what?! They could have annihilated you!" O'Neil exclaimed, says Sherman. Since Sherman believed in the quality and uniqueness of IBD's data, she felt totally comfortable talking to a group of market experts.

In the mid-1980s to early 1990s, the media finally began to recognize IBD's value to major players in the market. More business writers began to grasp why IBD's superior stock tables and emphasis on fast-growing companies, not lumbering giants, were helping readers make money. They began to see why IBD helped smart, busy readers make sound investment decisions. Consider the reader below, profiled in this article by the *Washington Times*:

> On his shoulders, William Clayton carries the weight of A Billion Four. That's $1,400,000,000, the approximate value of the stock portfolio he manages as a senior vice president for the E.F. Hutton Group Inc.
>
> Hungry for data and starved for time, Mr. Clayton catches up with the previous day's financial news by reading a business newspaper during his 45-minute, chauffeured commute to Manhattan from his home in Short Hills, N.J.
>
> The name of the paper? The *Wall Street Journal*, of course, you say. But you're wrong. For his early-morning reading, Mr. Clayton prefers a 36-page, 3-year-old sheet out of Los Angeles called *Investor's Daily*, whose brash publisher hopes to attract 800,000 readers—about 749,000 more than it now has.
>
> —Kevin McManus, "Investor's Daily carving a niche in business news," page 8C

"O'Neil does seem to have invented a better mousetrap," Jack Egan wrote in an Oct. 28, 1991, column in *U.S. News & World Report*. Egan pointed out that the tables displayed the EPS Rating and the RS Rating first before typical data such as the high, low and closing prices of the previous session. "The stock tables reflect O'Neil's conviction that winners can be identified on the basis of price 'momentum'—stocks with demonstrated earnings records that climb faster than the market" (page 87).

"I still read the *Wall Street Journal* for its articles," Robert J. Farrell, chief market analyst at Merrill Lynch, told *BusinessWeek* in a Dec. 21, 1987, article. "But I much prefer *Investor's Daily* as an investment tool" (page 121).

O'Neil was even more blunt.

"The *Journal* is archaic compared to what you get here," Ed Moosbrugger quoted O'Neil as saying in the *Daily Breeze*, a Torrance, Calif.–based regional paper, on Nov. 22, 1992.

He could back this up with the paper's circulation gains. In March 1986, the first period that the Audit Bureau of Circulations counted IBD's circ, the paper had 40,806 subscribers. Two years later, by March 1988, that number had more than doubled to 102,844. From March 1986 to September 1992, IBD's circ grew 268% to 150,075. Meanwhile, the *Journal's* circ fell 10% from 1,985,559 to 1,795,206.

Interestingly, O'Neil's jab came after the *Journal* revised its market coverage by adding a third section on Oct. 3, 1988, called "Money and Investing." In the tables, the *Journal* used bold type and underlining to highlight big price changes. The *New York Times* and other dailies wrote that newspaper analysts thought the *Journal* was beginning to acknowledge IBD's way of organizing market data to help investors make better decisions. "Clearly, that third section is aimed at *Investor's Daily*," Edward Atorino, Smith Barney newspaper analyst, said in a Nov. 7, 1988, *Times* article. WSJ editors rebuffed such remarks.

# A Few Big Advertising Scores

At the start, not a few critics howled at IBD's lack of cutting-edge reporting. O'Neil and his team listened. IBD beefed up on technology coverage.

O'Neil had known many years earlier that technology stocks often supplied lots of wind in the market's sails. Before Microsoft, Dell and Cisco Systems came along, investors got to invest in giant tech winners such as Texas Instruments, which jumped out of an eight-month cup-with-handle base in March 1958 and grew 728% in 28 months; Prime Computer, which broke out of a cup-with-handle base in early 1978 and vaulted 1,500% in 40 months; and Wang Labs, which also burst out of a cup-with-handle formation around the same time as Prime Computer and leapt 1,543% in just 34 months.

On Sept. 15, 1998, IBD launched a front-page column called "Computers Made Plain." The goal? Teach readers the basics on various computing devices. Keep them on top of the latest tech trends changing the workplace and life at home. Meanwhile, IBD's Silicon Valley bureau, established in the early 1990s and now based in Sunnyvale, Calif., built a reputation for superior, detailed coverage of computer and telecom news.

The focus on technology has paid off in the form of advertising dollars. So did a unique advertising strategy.

Terri Chiodo nailed the Dell Computer ad account for IBD in 1995. It took her nearly four years of hard work and persistence, she says. Today, Dell remains a major advertiser.

After many phone calls, letters, and meetings with Dell's ad firm, Chiodo got a break. The man in charge of ads at Dell invited her to meet in Austin. As she grew to know the company better, she found that Dell was different from other tech companies. Ad agencies tended to avoid risk. They didn't push their clients to spend money in newer, smaller, lesser known publications. Dell, however, measured the cost of its advertising per sale of each personal computer. It wanted to find low-cost advertising media because Dell prided itself as the low-cost pioneer in the PC industry.

Chiodo told the man that IBD would guarantee a 30% reduction in the cost per lead. If necessary, Dell could keep running ads in IBD free until that happened. Dell signed up. The Texas firm ran ads. It worked. Dell found IBD was the lowest-cost source of PC sales among the print media. An early test showed Dell got 150% more leads per dollar spent with IBD than with the *Wall Street Journal* and 250% more than the *New York Times*.

In the spring of 1998, IBD ran ads in *Ad Age* that drove the *Wall Street Journal* up the wall. It said that a 1994 study showed "IBD pulled 23% of the leads with only 11% of the *Journal*'s circulation at the time. Today with 14.5% of the *Journal*'s circulation, IBD's pull would equal 30%." The ad pointed out that the *Journal* kept raising its ad rates despite declining circulation. It also noted the following facts:

1. 15.3% of IBD readers were CEOs, higher than the *Journal*'s 12.9%.

2. The CPM (cost to reach 1,000 readers) for IBD was $95.33 versus $195.59 for the *Journal* (source: 1997 survey, Monroe Mendelsohn).

3. 75% of IBD readers do not read the *Journal* (source: Readex, Inc.).

"If Dell can sell its computers two or three times as efficiently in IBD as in the *Journal*, it follows that you can probably sell your product and increase your brand awareness for substantially less money as well." After getting complaints for many months from the WSJ, Dell officials later called Chiodo and asked her to pull the ad.

Kathy Sherman sold what she called "The IBD Difference" to Leo Burnett, the Chicago ad giant in charge of the United Airlines accounts, and to Bozell's agency in Texas for the American Airlines accounts. Sherman showed what exactly made IBD stand apart from the *Journal*. They got it. "The woman for the United Airlines account asked me, 'Why doesn't the *Journal* have an Earnings Per Share rating in its stock tables?' " Sherman said.

IBD also sealed ad contracts with Cadillac, Mercedes Benz, Infiniti and Nissan with this strategy as well. They all recognized that the IBD readership was affluent, enthusiastic about the paper and distinct from those who took the *Journal*. A 1998 Readex, Inc., survey found that 83%—**that's right, 83%**—of all IBD readers did not read the *Journal*. Luxury car makers realized they could not ignore the IBD audience.

## A New IBD Star Is Born

No doubt, David Ryan helped grow the paper's popularity in the late 1980s to early 1990s.

As a teenager, Ryan waited in line at O'Neil's Stock Mart bookshop to get his weekly fill of stock charts in a publication still known today as *Daily Graphs*. Then one day, Ryan knocked on O'Neil's door and asked for a job, any job. After mastering O'Neil's strategy on how to select, buy and sell great stocks, Ryan soared to national fame by winning the U.S. Investing Championships, an event hosted by Stanford University professor Norm Zadeh, three years in a row. From 1985 through the end of 1987, Ryan amassed a 1,379% net gain in his own portfolio. The result was verified by Ryan's monthly account statements. He became a key in-house money manager for William O'Neil + Co. In addition, *Money* magazine, the *Journal* and other publications featured him and the IBD way of buying stocks, which even today sounds contrary to conventional wisdom.

Meanwhile, in February 1988, O'Neil published "How to Make Money in Stocks: A Winning System in Good Times and Bad." It was timely. The Black Monday Crash of Oct. 19, 1987, had rattled investors, yet the market recovered well.

The book took years to write. It's a testament to O'Neil's belief that facts help investors in the market, not opinions from neighbors, friends, or the latest talking head on TV.

To further help investors, O'Neil wrote more books on how to identify the market's direction and how to buy and sell great stocks by using IBD ratings and charts. (See Figures 1.1 and 1.2.) Countless seminars hosted by O'Neil helped yield a bumper crop of David Ryan-like investors across the country.

The books underscored O'Neil's desire to educate the public on several truths about the market that shot down the conventional wisdom:

1.  It takes hard work and dedication to find great winners.

2.  Investors can achieve great results by following the CAN SLIM™ Investment Research Tool(s) method developed by O'Neil, not by relying on biased or faulty recommendations of pundits, analysts or friends.

3.  Buy high, sell higher: Great stocks begin their runs by shooting out to new highs, not by plunging to new lows. Buying shares of Polaroid, Xerox and other former leading stocks at new lows long after they have made their price peaks is a recipe for disaster.

4.  Charts aren't ouija-board nonsense; they simply illustrate the balance of supply and demand in a stock and the daily decision making of millions of investors

5.  Losing stocks should be sold quickly. Winning stocks should be held as long as possible until they show signs of a real top.

6.  Without having a set of sound sell rules, unsuspecting investors will eventually lose all their profits and possibly take huge losses.

When they have applied these truths to their investments, even independent investing bodies have reproduced the same kind of success that O'Neil, Ryan and O'Neil's other top money managers have achieved.

The American Association of Individual Investors' (AAII) real-time study of dozens of investment styles and strategies showed that IBD's CAN SLIM method produced a 704.9% gain from 1998 to 2003. In contrast, the S&P 500 eked out a 14.6% gain as the six-year study spanned one of the worst bubble market crashes in all of mankind.

It goes to show that many individual readers can achieve the success that Ryan had. The AAII study used real-time stock trades and analysis; it did not back-test past stock performances. The method also achieved gains every year during that six-year period.

How did it do so well in the bear market conditions that existed from 2000 to 2002, when most stocks got beaten up? O'Neil says he believes that through its study the AAII discovered many small banks that were jumping out of their bases and hitting new highs. These regional lenders benefited from the Federal Reserve's 13 cuts in interest rates and the housing boom that followed. Home building stocks also bucked the bear market, making new highs from 2000 to 2002.

Testimonials also have served as evidence that IBD has taught readers a system of investing that maximizes gains, minimizes losses and forces them to invest at the right time—specifically, when the market is riding a solid uptrend. Since roughly three out of four stocks follow the market's trend, buying the best quality stocks at the start of a new bull market increases an investor's chance of success.

"The impact itself is the real story behind *Investor's Business Daily*. 'Oh, you've changed my life.' We hear this so much it's almost a broken record. I've heard that hundreds of times, not just once or twice," said Sherman. "IBD is an empowering tool."

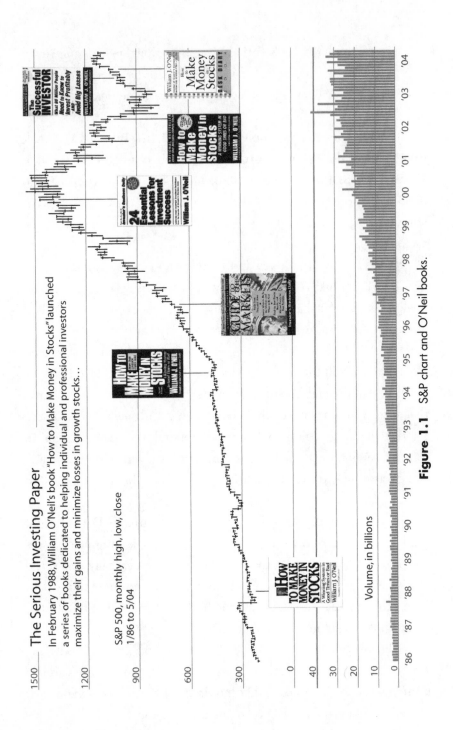

## The Serious Investing Paper

In February 1988, William O'Neil's book "How to Make Money in Stocks" launched a series of books dedicated to helping individual and professional investors maximize their gains and minimize losses in growth stocks....

S&P 500, monthly high, low, close
1/86 to 5/04

Volume, in billions

**Figure 1.1** S&P chart and O'Neil books.

...the mainstream press, meanwhile, offered a broader menu.

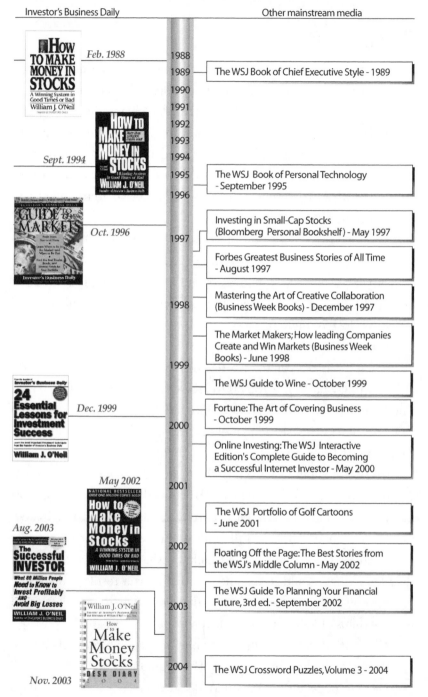

**Figure 1.2** Comparison between books published by IBD and books published by other business presses.

## Riding the Bear

In the spring of 2000, IBD unveiled its biggest advertising campaign yet. The roaring bull market of the late 1990s helped boost IBD's circulation. O'Neil saw this as a chance to make a big jump on the *Journal*. IBD hired Young & Rubicam, and together they came up with catchy phrases such as "IBD—Don't read it, use it." Posters were plastered all over Manhattan's billboards and buses. TV commercials ran during the Oscars, the NCAA college basketball tournament and other prime-time events.

The advertising appeared to work—for a while. IBD's circulation rose 11% from about 274,000 in March 2000 to 304,000 in September of that year, according to figures from the Audit Bureau of Circulations (ABC). During the same period, the *Journal's* circulation fell nearly 3% to 1.76 million.

Then the bear unleashed its fury.

When it was all over, the Nasdaq dropped 78% from its March 10, 2000, intraday peak of 5,132.50 to an October 2002 low of 1,108.40. The S&P 500 shed 51%, the Dow industrial average 39%. It was the worst decline in U.S. stock market history since the Dow caved 89.5% from August 1929 to July 1932.

IBD's circ fell in lock step. In the March 2003 period, circ was at 242,661, down 20% from the peak. IBD took the circulation figure off its masthead in late March 2001. Part of the decline was anticipated, as IBD launched eIBD, its fully online version, in order to serve its core readers in key regions in a timelier fashion. Executives say that they knew they would lose some circulation as a result of spending fewer resources in geographic areas that proved extremely costly and were perhaps of less value to its advertisers.

The *Wall Street Journal*, meanwhile, managed to raise its circ to 1,820,600, the highest in five years. How could that be?

The gap between IBD's and WSJ's "official" circ figures perhaps would have been smaller if the *Journal* and a few other big papers had

NAYSAYERS AND NERVOUS RIVALS

not been able to get the ABC to allow certain types of arrangements to be added to circ, O'Neil argues. Based on his research, O'Neil claims IBD had previously taken market share from the WSJ almost every year. But the *Journal* had steadily offset eroding circulation for full-price subscriptions by boosting heavily discounted sales to students, hotels, and airlines. IBD also once offered discounts to students and investing bodies, but at a much smaller scale, such as striking deals with universities. IBD research has found that Dow Jones & Co., the *Journal's* owner, even counts discounted papers available to thousands of its employees as official circ, thus padding the total. These accounting practices continue today.

"Because of all the ABC rule changes made in the last five years to accommodate some of the bigger publishers, our research indicates the WSJ lost about 400,000 regular circulation on top of the approximate 300,000 lost from the prior 15 years, and replaced it with softer circ from these new methods that ABC rules now allowed," O'Neil said.

The more than two years from March 1998 to December 2000 are telling. Newsstand sales in that period fell 18% to 178,357, according to the *Wall Street Journal* Statement of Total Circulation. Full-price subscriptions declined 20% to 1.04 million.

Yet total circulation dipped by only 359 copies if you apply audit bureau rules to the *Journal's* December Statement of Total Circulation.

Hotels, airlines, students and the company's own employees pad the total. They pay as little as 50% of the cover price.

Consider the travel industry component. These are the papers you might find in your hotel room, airline seat or rental car. They're charged to you in the fine print of your bill. The number of single copies sold for half-price through hotels, airlines and car agencies soared 2,541% to 77,659 from 2,940.

On top of these discounted single-copy sales, the latest period included 526,957 subscriptions sold at less than the basic price. They're up 74% from 1998.

Who's subscribing to the *Journal* on the cheap?

One group is employees. They take 17,666 papers, up 76% from 1998, the audit bureau says. The *Journal* employed only 1,897 of Dow Jones' 8,574 workers at year-end 2000. The rest of the subscriptions could come from retirees and part-time workers such as newspaper carriers, which the ABC allows to be counted in this category.

Students make up a big chunk of discounted subscribers; 135,638 pay half price, a 9% slice of the subscriber base.

—From Steve Watkins, "Eroding Journal Circulation Lurks Behind Dow Jones' Current Woes," April 10, 2001, IBD

The debate over circulation accounting practices intensified in June 2004. The Tribune Publishing Company said that, based on an internal audit and an audit by the ABC, its New York–based *Newsday* had overstated its circulation. The paper's vice president of circulation admitted that some free copies of the newspaper had been counted as paid circulation. In July, *Newsday*'s publisher resigned.

## The Online Generation: More Than Simply Subscribing to IBD

IBD's Web site, investors.com, has 350,000 registered users and ranks as one of the most frequently used financial Web sites in terms of the number of hits per registered user. Marketing officials estimate IBD has a total audience of about 800,000.

Readers have also found a new resource to learn about how the market really works—other IBD readers.

As of May 17, 2004, nearly 17,000 investors have signed up to attend International IBD Meetups worldwide. At these shindigs, IBD readers meet with fellow readers to discuss stocks, learn from each other's successes and failures, and sharpen skills on how to buy and sell stocks correctly. They span the globe from Denver to Toronto to Copenhagen, Denmark. Of that number, 521 cities throughout the world are presently hosting or have signed up to host International IBD Meetups. Here are the top 10 locations and their respective participation counts:

| Rank | Location | Members as of May 17, 2004 |
| --- | --- | --- |
| 1. | New York City | 482 |
| 2. | Orange County, Calif. | 347 |
| 3. | Houston, Tex. | 345 |
| 4. | Santa Clara County, Calif. | 315 |
| 5. | Dallas-Plano, Tex. | 307 |
| 6. | Detroit, Mich. | 300 |
| 7. | Phoenix, Ariz. | 285 |
| 8. | Denver, Colo. | 242 |
| 9. | Philadelphia, Pa. | 206 |
| 10. | Northern N.J. | 200 |

I about fainted (okay, I exaggerate) when I got the e-mail suggesting that there were actually enough people to have a meet-up in Tallahassee and that Friday's was the suggested place.

—rhr, posted on IBD Forums message board,
investors.com, March, 3, 2004

IBD has clearly achieved a loyal following among readers who themselves are savvy, smart and successful. The 2004 IBD Subscriber Study, which as of June 2004 was being audited by the ABC, confirms this. Consider the following:

41.3% have a net worth of $1 million or more.

80.5% of readers are career professionals or hold managerial titles.

27.9% are CEOs.

More than 75% read four or five of the last five issues of IBD.

Nearly 8 out of 10 had saved an article for future reference.

64% said that IBD is more useful than the WSJ (of those who regularly read WSJ).

92% use the Internet to track investments.

72.7% had visited IBD's Web site.

IBD may never become the largest investing publication. But no one would argue with the fact that it has helped dedicated readers make big strides in the market and avoid devastating losses.

**O'Neil's office.** William O'Neil, founder and chairman of *Investor's Business Daily*, sits at his desk in the IBD headquarters office in west Los Angeles. Standing behind him (from left to right) are Tony Jones, customer service manager, and Ralph Perrini, vice president and marketing manager.

**The management team of IBD.** *From left to right, back row:* Chris Gessel, executive editor; Wes Mann, editor in chief; Joseph Swantek, direct marketing manager; Jessica Jensen, senior vice president of new product and business development; William O'Neil, chairman; Jerry Polk, senior vice president of production and circulation; Jamila Khalil, manager of classified ads/Investor's NewsWire; Steve Souder, director of human resources; Margo Schuster, vice president of customer relations; Eugene Kumamoto, chief financial officer; Susan Warfel, managing editor.

*From left to right, first row:* Kathleen Sherman, vice president, director of corporate communications; Karen Anderson, executive vice president; Harlan Ratzky, vice president of Internet marketing; Terri Chiodo, vice president and national advertising director; Rajneesh Gupta, vice president of technology; Heather Davis, vice president, director of research; David Sharpe, senior vice president of Financial and Strategic Planning; Doug Fuller, vice president, circulation.

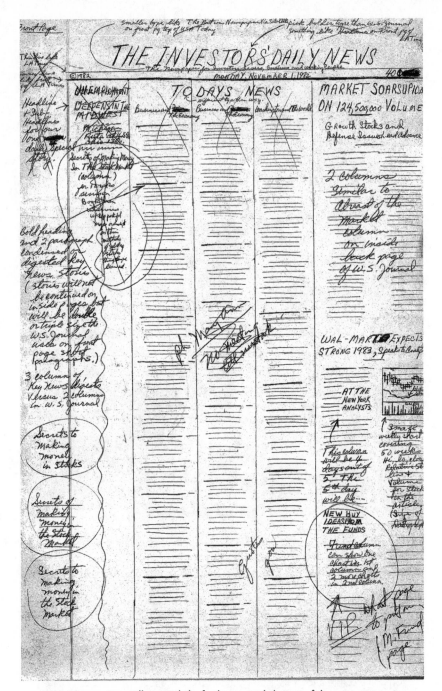

**IBD blueprint.** Bill O'Neil drafted an initial design of the newspaper in November 1982 while vacationing at a cabin in Oregon. He drew in blue pen 20 pages on a yellow legal pad. This was the first page.

**Terry Jones** used the Hastech computerized editing system when the paper was launched in April 1984. IBD employed state-of-the-art "computer-to-plate" technology that saved costs and labor.

**IBD launch.** IBD staffers celebrate the paper's national launch on April 9, 1984.

**William O'Neil** created the first computerized stock database in the U.S., and in 1963 he formed an institutional research and brokerage firm. Today, the large weekly books of Datagraphs, which contain data on 130 fundamental and technical variables on each stock, are used by more than 400 institutional investors including J.P. Morgan, Merrill Lynch Asset Management, Fidelity, John Hancock Advisors, the United Nations, Wachovia Bank and Tennessee Consolidated Retirement Systems.

The *Investor's Business Daily* **headquarters** in Playa Vista, west Los Angeles, on a Saturday morning. IBD also has bureaus in Sunnyvale, Calif., New York and Washington D.C.

## Investor's Business Daily

# Real People. Real Success.

**Ms. Florence Rutherford and
Dr. Frances Jones**
Individual Investors

**How Rutherford and Jones read *IBD*:**

- First we look at "The Real Most Active." It focuses on stocks with the most trading activity and discusses why they're moving. We study them and go with the best.

- "The Best Ups" and "New Highs" lists are great stocks to also study. We pick the ones with outstanding earnings growth and earnings potential. These features brought America Online to our attention two years ago.

- Then we look at the stock charts in *IBD*'s sister publication, Daily Graphs. Over time we learned what good graphs look like.

- The IBD *Smart Select*™ Corporate Ratings narrow down our choices by eliminating the mediocre stocks for us.

*These Texas twins have more in common than just their looks. They have put their heads together to earn a +57.7% compounded annual return for 11 years. Their portfolios mirror one of those "Biggest Winners" lists you see every quarter or so. They talked with* Investor's Business Daily *about how they do it:*

**What do you attribute to your consistent success?**

"We discovered that *IBD* gives you the fundamental and technical information necessary to choose outstanding stocks. Other business publications don't provide information like Industry Group Relative Price Strength Rating, Earnings Per Share Rating, Sales+Profit Margins+ROE Rating, Volume % Change and more. This information is vital for investors who want to make *informed* investment decisions."

**What would you suggest to new investors?**

"If you want the knowledge and research necessary for a winning portfolio, read *Investor's Business Daily* every day. Founder William J. O'Neil's book, *How to Make Money in Stocks*, and *Investor's Business Daily*'s free educational tape are an excellent start in learning to invest intelligently."

**To subscribe, call**
## 800-831-2525

### Investor's Business Daily
FOR PEOPLE WHO CHOOSE TO SUCCEED

## Changing readers' lives.

In a long-running campaign titled "Real People, Real Success," IBD profiled many readers who benefited from the ease of using stock ratings that simply ranged from 1 to 99 and from learning how to analyze stock charts.

# CHAPTER 2

# Changing
# Readers' Lives

## IBD's Secret Sauce

My goal is to help as many men and women as possible discover how to get ahead by saving and investing. . . . The strategies I recommend are the same strategies I use and have used for the past 30 years.

—William O'Neil, "How to Make
Money in Stocks," February 1988

**Q:** How many people have become millionaires thanks to IBD?

**A:** A lot more than Publisher's Clearing House. My wild guess is anywhere from 500 to 5,000, or maybe more . . .

—William O'Neil

The *Los Angeles Times* raked in five Pulitzer Prizes in 2004. As widely expected, the crosstown paper IBD got none.

The *LA Times* won awards for its coverage of the raging Southern California wild fires; for an "engrossing examination of the tactics that have made Wal-Mart the largest company in the world with cascading effects across American towns and developing countries," says the Pulitzer Prize Board's Web site (www.pulitzer.org); and for criticism, editorial writing and feature photography. It's now won at least one Pulitzer for seven straight years.

The *Wall Street Journal* also took home some of the hardware, grabbing a Pulitzer in the explanatory reporting category and one for beat reporting. It's now bagged at least one Pulitzer for six years in a row. Meanwhile, IBD's streak of not a single Pulitzer prize extended to 20 years in a row!

IBD might never win the journalism industry's top prize. Why? It has good writers, yet its feature articles are short. The writing style is punchy, not flowery. It can't send 200 writers and photographers to cover wildfires, earthquakes or floods. And its editorials stick out in a chiefly liberal news media world.

So why has IBD survived after slugging it out against a boatload of media giants—among them, *Barron's, BusinessWeek, Forbes, Fortune, Money* magazine and the *Journal*?

That's easy. The paper has helped thousands of investors make a lot of money. You don't need a judging committee to conclude that.

IBD got off the ground that way. O'Neil reaped huge profits in *two stocks*—yes, just two. Those gains secured the financial base for IBD. A pair of retail chains, Price Co. and Pic-N-Save, both soared more than 1,500% from the start of their biggest price moves. Over a 7½-year period beginning in 1976, O'Neil bought shares of Pic-N-Save, which was thinly traded back then, on 285 different days!

What fueled his conviction?

Continuously strong growth, year over year and quarter over quarter, in earnings and sales. An innovative concept, at the time, of selling all sorts of everyday items at low cost. Pretax margins, return on equity, annual earnings growth and a long-term debt-to-equity ratio all superior to that of Wal-Mart at the time. Last but not least, powerful stock-price action. At one point, O'Neil owned 4.99% of the total stock outstanding. (O'Neil never dared to go above 5%, which then would have required him to register his holdings with the SEC.) When he finally sold all his shares, the earliest holdings yielded a roughly 20-fold gain. O'Neil made a bundle.

As for Price Co., which had started out with just two stores in San Diego, those shares shot up more than 1,600% from 1982 to 1986. William O'Neil + Co. began buying shares when it broke out of its first base and headed for new highs. At one point, the firm held 3.6% of shares outstanding. O'Neil hit another home run. Price Co. later went on to become Costco Wholesale (COST), one of the largest discount chains in the world.

## Hard Work and Skill, Not Luck

How did O'Neil find these big winners and buy them at the right time?

As a young man, O'Neil bought a library of 2,000 books on the market. Most of them stank. Only a few were good. O'Neil learned that to make the truly big money, you need to find the true leaders, the one or two rare gems in the market that made exceptional gains. To find these big winners, O'Neil studied every stock in Jack Dreyfus' mutual fund in the late 1950s because Dreyfus proved to be one of the best stock pickers of his time. O'Neil studied the fundamentals and price behavior of these stocks as they shot to 52-week or all-time highs. He checked out the industry group performance of each of these market stars. Then he analyzed other great stocks that preceded Price Co. and Pic-N-Save.

Back in the early 1960s, conducting this study took some ingenuity. O'Neil hired a team of computer engineers and bought an IBM mainframe computer. He collected reams of data on each of these big winning stocks. What were profits like? What was return on equity?

How were pretax and after-tax margins? How about sales? Is inventory turnover high? How much long-term debt is on the books? How old were these firms? How long have their CEOs been around? What was the level of trading volume like when these stocks rose in price? When they went down? What industry did they belong to? How did the industry itself perform in the market compared to its peers? You get the picture.

Through all this hard work, the Oklahoma native unearthed a law of the market: The very best growth stocks typically show a top-flight record of profit growth, sales growth and stock-price strength *before* they suddenly soar to new highs and make their biggest moves. Yes, great stocks must show their business greatness first before they take off on the longest leg of their price rallies. He found that this pattern repeats over and over, from one bull market to the next. Perhaps no one else—in the U.S., at least—had done this before.

O'Neil found his edge.

## A Continuous Cycle of Terrific Retail and Consumer Stocks

Price Co. and Pic-N-Save weren't the first great retail and consumer-oriented stocks. O'Neil saw the same cycle of profit growth and investor greed begin with Interstate Department Stores and Korvette in 1960, Kmart in 1964 and with Jack Eckerd Drug in 1967. Many more have followed. In the 1970s and 1980s, Levitz Furniture, Wal-Mart (WMT), Home Depot (HD), Limited (LTD), Circuit City (CC) and others made upward strides of 1,000% to 20,000% or more. In the late 1980s to 1990s, they passed the baton to Kohl's (KSS) and Gap (GPS). In recent years Chico's FAS (CHS), Coach (COH), Urban Outfitters (URBN), International Game Technology (IGT) and for-profit school chain Apollo Group (APOL) have also logged tremendous gains.

The next challenge for O'Neil was to convince the big guns of the market—the mutual funds, pension funds, insurance firms, banks, hedge funds and the like—that his discovery could help them make money and beat their peers. After becoming the youngest person to own a seat on the New York Stock Exchange, O'Neil founded William O'Neil + Co. in 1964. He later started another company, O'Neil Data Systems (ODS), to print his stock research. Today, more than 400 of the largest institutional investors subscribe to O'Neil's stock research service. They include names you've heard of: Fidelity Investments, American Express, J.P. Morgan, Merrill Lynch, John Hancock Advisers, SwissRe, SunTrust Banks, the United Nations, the YMCA Retirement Fund, British Airway Pension Funds, Tennessee Consolidated Retirement Systems and the State of Wisconsin Investment Board. The key service is William O'Neil Direct Access, or WONDA®, which gives institutional clients access to the O'Neil Database®. This consists of charts of stocks that also contain 126 separate pieces of data about each company. Ninety-eight pieces of the data cover a stock's fundamentals, and 28 involve the stock's chart action, or technicals. Every week, many subscribers also get two heavy books, each about 600 pages, filled with perhaps the most data-crammed charts on the planet.

> Bill has an ability to see through conventional wisdom and be completely unencumbered by it, unlike most people. He just figures things out for himself, which is why his products are unique.
>
> —Chris Gessel, executive editor, IBD

## Helping the Little Guy

On Wall Street, some people say, you have retail money and institutional money. The retail money is invested for the most part by individual investors such as you or your neighbor or coworker, and it tends to make up a lot of the trades executed during the first half-hour of the day. The institutional money is invested by organized players such as mutual funds, hedge funds, corporate and government pension funds, insurers, university endowments and banks, and they buy and sell by the tens or hundreds of thousands of shares throughout the trading session.

O'Neil refused to think of the market's players in those terms. In 1983, he lamented over how individual investors lacked the information and understanding critical to do well on Wall Street. Papers across the country, including the WSJ, used the same tables from the Associated Press that contained data such as P-E ratios, dividend yield and 52-week lows. These tables left a sour taste in O'Neil's mouth. These data had not helped him discover the best stocks over the previous three decades. The small investor deserved better. One day, on a plane thousands of feet above Earth, one of his senior executives, Al Mac-Gregor, suggested, "Why don't we start a newspaper since our computer data are more helpful than what's in the WSJ. Let's put it to good use," according to Kathy Sherman, IBD's head of PR. O'Neil rejected the idea more than once. But over time, he became convinced a brand-new newspaper could fill a need. He decided to go for it.

An epiphany occurred. A quest began.

When *Investor's Daily* (before it became *Investor's Business Daily* on Sept. 16, 1991) began rolling off the presses in Los Angeles on April 9, 1984, O'Neil did something radical. He took mundane stock tables—those dull, lifeless strips of data that business editors and newsroom assistants thought existed only to be torn off the AP teletype machine—and turned them into roadmaps to wealth.

IBD's tables featured the *Earnings Per Share Rating*, which ranged from 1 to 99. If a stock had a 99, that meant its earnings growth over the past three to five years and in the two most recent quarters was superior to 99% of all public companies. Today, the EPS Rating also gauges the stability of a firm's earnings, or how steady its profit was from quarter to quarter, year to year. Imagine tons of institutional equity research compressed into a numerical rating so easy to use that school kids could pick stocks like the best pros. Many IBD readers have commented that this system makes it simple to find out which companies are growing the fastest. In general, most of the biggest market winners during bull market cycles over the past 50 years scored an EPS Rating of at least 80 before they broke out to all-time price highs and made their big moves. The very best ones had an EPS Rating of 90 to 99, O'Neil says.

IBD's tables featured another new tool for the stock picker's toolbox: The *Relative Price Strength Rating*. This ranking also spans from 1 to 99 and measures a stock's price strength over the past 12 months. In an IBD study of the biggest market winners from the early 1950s to 2000, O'Neil found that the average RS Rating was 87 before they made their biggest price runs. In other words, strong stocks tend to get even stronger! O'Neil discovered that a stock that is rising faster than the market makes a habit of continuing to rise until a fundamental shift occurs in the supply and demand for the stock. In this sense, stock market behavior is similar to Isaac Newton's first law of motion: Every object in a state of uniform motion tends to remain in that state of motion unless an external force is applied to it.

Back then, most investors nosed their way through the stock tables of the *Journal* or their local paper to find out how their stock did the previous day. These stock tables were passive. *Investor's Business Daily's* stock tables were (and still are) proactive. The trick to using them: Circle the stocks that had high EPS and RS Ratings, say, 80 or higher. Also circle those with a Composite Rating of 90 or better. Add them to a watch list. If a stock gained 1 point or more in price, it would be boldfaced and maybe worth circling as well. That made it easier for readers—any reader, from the corporate CEO to grade-school kids—to spot the leading stocks, the real wealth generators of the market.

The percent increase in earnings per share has been proven in a major 30-year study of best-performing stocks to be the most important common variable in those successful moves—considerably more important than dividends or price-earnings ratios.

—"How To Read Tables" legend,
inaugural issue of IBD, April 9, 1984

## From Acorns Grow Big Oaks

For proof, consider Cisco Systems (CSCO), the greatest stock of the 1990s and one of the biggest wealth makers in U.S. market history.

The mass media all but ignored Cisco back in 1990, when it was still a tiny company based in Menlo Park, Calif. It made expensive networking gear called *routers*. These boxlike devices enabled computers in different locales to talk to each other. The U.S. military used these pearls of American ingenuity to communicate with field commanders in Iraq during the Persian Gulf War.

Although the company itself was still small, Cisco's stock flashed the kind of strength reminiscent of a Pic-N-Save and other past winners. Cisco had a product that has fundamentally changed the way we communicate, do business and get information. Today, with annual revenue north of $20 billion, it's made a huge impact on the growth of the world economy and the jobs market. These are the kinds of stocks that IBD has helped readers find when they're still young and growing fast, well before the masses find them.

On Oct. 18, 1990, the fifth day of a new market rally attempt, the major indexes bolted higher. The S&P 500 rose 2.3% and the Nasdaq 2.2% on a surge in volume on both the NYSE and the Nasdaq. This action, called a *follow-through*, confirmed that a new bull market was taking hold. That same day, Cisco roared out of what the great trader Jesse Livermore dubbed the "Shakeout + 3 points" chart pattern. It surged 2¼ points, or 9.3%, to 26.50. Volume ballooned to 421,000 shares, more than twice its average daily trade. In the Oct. 19 paper, Cisco stuck out in the OTC tables in boldfaced print (see Figure 2.1). It also showed up in the Over-The-Counter (OTC) daily market round-up article on the same page.

At the time of this breakout, it sported a 99 EPS Rating. This meant its year-over-year earnings growth over the past five years and in recent quarters was better than 99% of all public companies. Cisco belonged to an exclusive club of high-growth, innovation-savvy businesses. Its 82 RS Rating meant that over the past 12 months, it rose faster in price than 82 out of every 100 stocks in the market. The next day, Cisco kept moving higher, charging out of what is commonly known among serious IBD readers as a classic *double-bottom chart pattern* (see Figure 2.2).

Back then, just as he does now, O'Neil himself went through IBD's stock tables with a pen, circling stocks that had made big price moves, had high ratings and had seen dramatic spikes in volume. The new tables alone, however, were just one step in the process of finding awesome stocks. O'Neil also added a daily table of stocks that showed exactly which ones were truly moving and grooving.

While building his models of the best growth stocks in the 1960s, O'Neil discovered that the best stocks weren't necessarily those that traded the most in terms of sheer number of shares. He found that on the day when these leaders broke out of their bases and rocketed to 52-week highs, volume that day was two, three, or even four times higher than its average daily volume had been over the past 50 sessions. Some of them had an average volume of only 10,000 or 20,000 shares. No matter. More important was the size of the volume increase. This sudden change signaled institutional activity in a stock. O'Neil cares about what the institutions are doing because they make up roughly 80 cents out of every significant dollar moved on the Nasdaq and the Big Board.

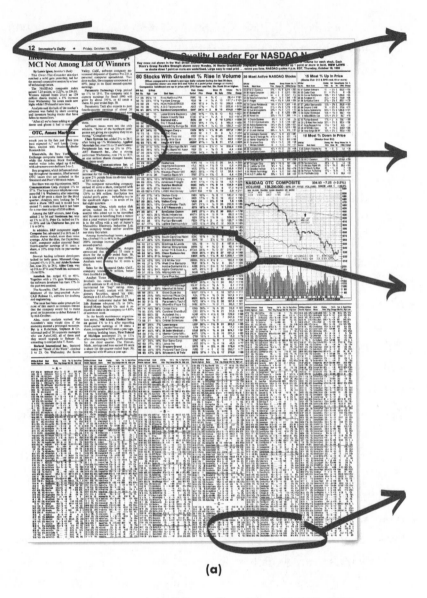

**(a)**

**Figure 2.1** (a) A full page from IBD on Oct. 19, 1990, when Cisco Systems broke out and began its huge rally; (b) Several areas of that page in zoomed-up format. Highlighter pen-like lines in red circle the key sections on the page.

**12** Investor's Daily ★ Friday, October 19, 1990

# Intel Anchors Strong Tech Group; MCI Not Among List Of Winners

Key ne Stock'

*A day after the stock market followed through with a 2.2% gain by the Nasdaq on Oct. 18, 1990, to begin a brand-new rally, IBD noted unusual strength.....*

## OTC, Amex Markets

smack you in the face just when you least expected it," said Laura Conigliaro, analyst with Prudential-Bache Research Inc.

Meanwhile, the New York Stock Exchange composite index rose 2.2%, while the American Stock Exchange market value index edged up 0.94%, with advancers over decliners 3-to-2.

Buy programs, which influenced trading throughout the session, lifted several OTC issues that are included in the

winners. Some of the hardware companies are giving me apoplexy they're so strong," Conigliaro said.

**Cisco Systems Inc.** added 2¼ to 26½ after being up 1¾ Wednesday. **Applied Materials Inc.** rose 2¼ to 23 and **Conner Peripherals Inc.** was up 2¼ to 19⅜. **AST Research Inc.**, also a strong performer Wednesday, rose 1⅝ to 18⅛ as one million shares changed hands, three times usual.

**SynOptics Communications Inc.** of Mountain View, Calif., jumped 3½ to 27½ after reporting a 173% profit increase for the third quarter. The issue

| | | |
|---|---|---|
| 81 | 87 | 2 |
| 78 | 75 | 1 |
| 31 | 47 | 5 |
| 88 | 39 | 3 |
| 92 | 92 | 7 |
| 37 | 39 | 2 |
| 95 | 50 | 2 |
| 37 | 39 | 2 |
| 95 | 42 | 2 |
| 50 | 80 | 1 |
| 84 | 69 | 2 |
| 96 | 74 | 2 |
| 75 | 52 | 4 |
| 76 | 70 | 4 |
| 83 | 67 | 3 |

*..... among tech stocks such as Cisco Systems, which rose 9% that day.*

*The stock was also highlighted in this table, now called "Where The Big Money's Flowing," because volume that day was more than twice its 50-day average.....*

*..... and was boldfaced here due to its high quality: a top-drawer 99 Earnings Per Share Rating and an 82 Relative Price Strength Rating. Cisco went on to gain more than 70,000% to its March 2000 peak.*

**(b)**

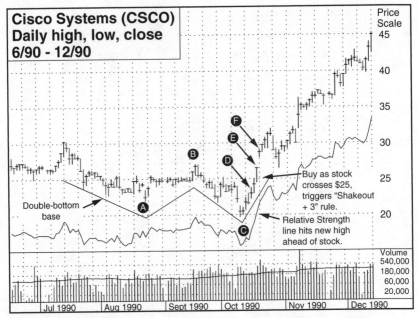

| **A** | Hits lowest point of $22 in first down leg of a double-bottom base. |
|---|---|
| **B** | Forms middle peak at $27, also crucial in a double bottom base. |
| **C** | Forms second down leg at $19.75. |
| **D** | Rises $1.38 to $23 on above-average volume on 10/16/90; boldfaced in OTC tables in next day's paper. |
| **E** | Appears in "80 Stocks With Greatest % Rise in Volume" table in the next day's paper. |
| **F** | Gaps out of a 14-week double-bottom base on its second highest volume ever; pivot point is $27.10, 10 cents above the middle peak. Appears in "OTC Stocks In The News" Charts page and was the second stock featured in the OTC market round-up. |

**Figure 2.2** The breakout. Chart of daily high, low, and close price bars of Cisco Systems in 1990.

Imagine a stock that has been swimming in a price range of between $30 and $40 a share for a few months. Then one day, the stock suddenly bursts past $40, to $41, $42 and finally closes at $43. Volume zooms to 1 million shares. If it normally trades 500,000 shares a day, then volume that session was twice, or 100%, higher than normal.

What does this action mean?

It means that institutional investors are falling over each other to grab shares. They've found a winner, and they want shares right here, right now. Their accumulation of thousands, even millions, of shares over weeks and months fuels a stock's breakout and long-term rally. Through the paper, IBD offered investors across America a front-row seat to this exciting action.

The April 9, 1984, debut issue of *Investor's Daily* ran three tables with this new thinking on how to interpret trading volume of any stock. At the top of the NYSE tables page, *Investor's Daily* unveiled its "20 Stocks With Greatest Rise In Volume." The name was as flashy as a tweed coat. But it lay above the standard table of 20 most active stocks, the same table found in practically every paper across the nation. A table of 15 stocks experiencing unusually heavy volume ran at the top of the OTC and the Amex section too.

Over the years, IBD expanded and improved the table. On Oct. 19, 1990, the day after Cisco broke out, it appeared in a table called "80 Stocks With Greatest % Rise In Volume." This screen hunted for stocks that were trading at least $12 a share and showed a price change, either up or down, of three-eighths of a point or more. There, Cisco Systems was listed as the 49th stock. In the table, Cisco was boldfaced because it rose in price and scored an 80 or higher for both EPS and RS Ratings. Number 50 on the list was another precious diamond—Amgen, which today remains a biotech powerhouse located in Southern California. (Please see Figure 2.1 again.)

"Every newspaper in the country showed the most active list, but it was the same old giant companies like IBM, AT&T and GM," O'Neil said. "I wanted to show the innovative new companies that represented the new America."

## Blending the Best of Both Worlds: Earnings Strength and Price Strength

The EPS and RS Ratings weren't the only unique features of IBD's stock market coverage.

IBD ran 90 small weekly charts of individual stocks: 30 stocks that traded on the NYSE, 30 on the Amex and 30 on the Over The Counter (OTC) exchange, now known as the "Nasdaq." The stock database of William O'Neil + Co. spit out the names of stocks that had hit 52-week highs the previous day or had seen a sharp increase in daily trading volume compared to their 50-day average. These charts showed roughly one year's worth of price-and-volume action. They appeared on three separate pages titled "Stocks In The News."

Excuse me? "Stocks In The News"? The feature's name certainly sounds strange. After all, none of these pages printed news stories. But these charts are extremely relevant. The market, back then as it does now, prices in the past and present and looks months ahead into the future. The best stocks often rally well ahead of any good news that gets announced and written up in the paper. It's the nature of the beast. These rallies show up first on a stock's price-and-volume chart. And if institutional investors truly are loading up on shares, it shows up in the form of a large spike in volume. In fact, "Stocks In The News" has an outstanding record of "reporting" those stocks that have a chance to become the next greatest winners and thus "the news" of the future. These charts, IBD's proprietary ratings and stock screens are the special sauce that makes IBD a unique, reliable tool to find great stocks.

## Witchcraft? Voodoo? Hocus Pocus? Ouija-Board Nonsense? Nope.

Ask professors at prestigious business schools on the East Coast and strategists at the biggest Wall Street firms for their view of charts, and many will say that they're bogus and meaningless. Yet IBD isn't only about charts. It places fundamentals first; if a company doesn't have robust growth in earnings and sales, if it lacks a solid return on equity, its chances of becoming a mega-stock are slim.

The WONDA institutional product provides more than 3,000 data items in its custom screening database, and well over more than half of them have to do with a company's actual business and its fundamentals, *not* its technicals. The Daily Graphs Custom Screen Wizard, which can be accessed on investors.com, is a simpler version for individual investors. Those who have made money by using IBD home in on the stocks with the best fundamentals and the best technicals. They also know to sell shares at or near the top of the stock's run by looking at the technical action alone, not to wait for the fundamentals to show signs of cracking. The best way to view the technical action? Use a daily or weekly chart.

O'Neil, at the age of 71, still makes it a mission to rid Wall Street of this misunderstanding. At a recent IBD advanced seminar, he unveiled a Datagraph of eBay. A few of the attendees stared in amazement. On the chart, which was already stuffed with details on the company's fundamentals, technical action and data on institutional sponsorship, were 66 handwritten items of notes by O'Neil that pointed out what in fact made eBay a great stock in 2003. He had studied the company by reading all 17 articles published in IBD from 2000 to the end of 2002. In October of that year, the bear finally went into hibernation after three years of clawing the market.

## Not All Charts Are the Same

Many brokers and companies that track stocks offer charts, some of them over the Internet and many of them free. But not all charts are the same. IBD's charts are not simply yearlong weekly charts that show a high, low and close for each week. Over the years, O'Neil has stuffed them with information including recent earnings and sales growth, EPS Rating, RS Rating, the Relative Strength line, the number of shares outstanding and a brief description of what exactly the firm does. O'Neil does not want readers to buy a stock solely on its price momentum. Is the company consistently growing profits at a fast rate? Does it have a truly innovative product that is changing people's lives or how they work? Is return on equity high? Is long-term debt low? Does it have strong management? All of these questions matter. That's why to this day, O'Neil continues to say 60% to 70% of a decision to buy a stock must be based on its fundamentals and 30% to 40% on its technicals.

Let's go back to Cisco. A day after roaring ahead 2.25 points on heavy volume on Oct. 18, Cisco gapped up another 2.25 points to mark a three-month high of 28.75. Volume zoomed to 837,400 shares, the second-highest level since its Feb. 16, 1990, IPO and 360% higher than its 50-day average daily volume. O'Neil's stock database spotted this unusual strength. In the next day's paper, Cisco showed up on the "OTC Stocks In The News" page (see Figure 2.3). *Cisco went on to gain roughly 70,000%.* A $10,000 investment in October 1990 would have grown to $7 million by its peak in March 2000 (see Figure 2.4).

## Time to Play the Devil's Advocate

At this point, it's fair to ask: "How could one possibly have known that this was the time to hunt for a great stock?"

Fair question. After all, Wall Street was suffering its first bear market of the 1990s. The Nasdaq slid 31%, from 470 in mid-July to a low of 322.93 on Oct. 12. Who would have had any confidence to buy any stock with the market plunging like that?

O'Neil would. It's not because of a gut feeling or because he likes to take wild risks. The reason is that the market itself flashed a signal that a new bull run was in the works. Excluding market bubbles, the

# New bull markets produce new stock stars

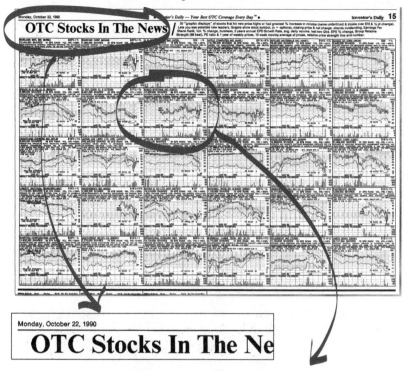

Cisco Systems surged out of a 14-week double-bottom base in strong trade on Friday, Oct. 19, 1990. Its weekly chart appeared on the "OTC Stocks In The News" page of IBD the following Monday, Oct. 22. The IBD chart also pointed out that Cisco was a "leading supplier" of networking products and boasted annual earnings-per-share growth of 262% over the past five years.

**Figure 2.3** Cisco weekly chart. New bull markets produce new stock stars.

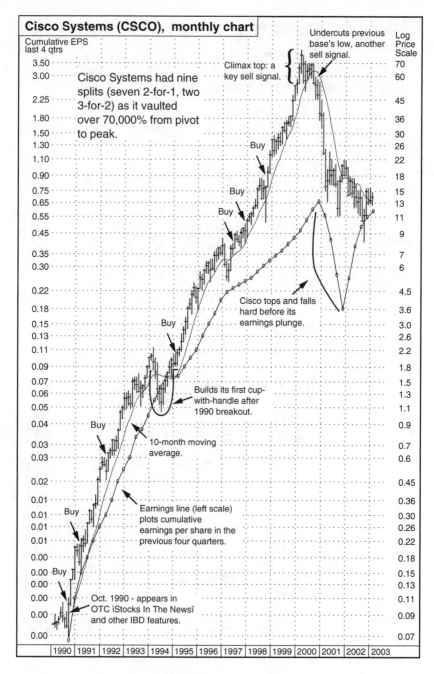

**Figure 2.4** Cisco monthly chart.

biggest stock gains are achieved by buying the leading stocks, the ones with the best growth, in the early years of a brand-new bull market.

How do you find this signal?

After the market has suffered a sharp decline, all the frightened and frustrated investors who have been thinking about selling eventually do so. But once they're gone, stocks start to rally because fresh demand for shares comes in. If institutional investors truly want to own stock, they'll hustle to grab those shares. As a result, the major indexes should repeatedly rise sharply on heavier volume than the prior session.

If you see a gain of roughly 1.7% or more among at least one of the major indexes—the Nasdaq, S&P 500 or Dow—coming on the 4th through 10th day of a new rally attempt and volume is higher, take note of it. In IBD parlance, such a day is called a *follow-through*. Not all follow-throughs work, but more than three out of every four do, and *every major bull market in the past 100 years began with one.* Some follow-throughs are huge, such as the 3.9% gain on March 17, 2003. That year, the Nasdaq gained 50%.

Let's return to October 1990. On the 12th, the Nasdaq slipped nearly 1% during the session but closed with a 0.6% gain on lower turnover than the previous session. Nice reversal. That's Day 1 of a new rally attempt. Four sessions later, the Nasdaq thrust ahead 2.2% on volume of 139.3 million shares, 14% higher than the previous day and well above its average volume over the past 50 sessions. It was a picture-perfect follow-through. That same day, Oct. 18, was the day of Cisco's breakout and beginning of a 10-year rally.

October 1990 was indeed a scary time to buy stocks. President George H. W. Bush had announced plans to go to war with Iraq and drive Saddam Hussein out of Kuwait. The Gulf War was about to become reality. Stocks had been plummeting in the preceding few months. The Dow Jones industrial average had fallen 22.5% from July to early October that year. The Nasdaq had sunk 31%.

In September 1990, the percentage of bearish stock newsletter writers tracked by Investors Intelligence catapulted to 56%. Bullish writers slumped to 28%. Yet the market has shown time after time that bull markets are born in a sea of fear. Virtually every investor who was itching to sell stocks has sold. To perhaps ease their bruised egos, they too became bearish about the market, despite the fact that they don't own any stocks! But at market extremes, the crowd is usually wrong. With no more anxious sellers around, bargain-hunting buyers step in and push prices higher. Most folks are still afraid, but that fear eventually melts away as the rally gains steam. The market's cycle of hope, greed and fear starts all over again.

## Where's Everyone Else?

If Cisco was the new star of the market universe, the mainstream business media seemed to be orbiting Neptune. In the Oct. 20, 1990, "Business Day" page of the *New York Times*, the big news was that crude oil futures had dropped by more than 3 bucks a barrel to the lowest price in a month. The *New York Times'* "Business Digest" column printed five briefs on Midway Airlines, Zenith Electronics, Bank of New England, Texas Instruments, and B. Manischewitz, which agreed to a $42 million buyout by investment firm KKR & Co., and the firm's own management.

There wasn't a word about Cisco.

In fact, based on an article search by nexis.com, Cisco appeared *just six times* in the *New York Times* in all of 1990. It got a mention in the last sentence of a 443-word article focusing on the sudden resignation of the CEO of Vitalink Communications Corp, which made devices called *bridges* to link local area networks of personal computers. Two other *Times* articles spent one line mentioning Cisco's plan to sell 2.8 million shares in its initial public offering (IPO) on Feb. 16, 1990. The *Times'* other three mentions weren't in articles but in simple tables that gave Cisco's results in the fiscal quarters ended in April, July and October that year.

The *New York Times* seems to have been oblivious to the rise of Cisco until March 12, 1991, when Andrew Pollack wrote a feature on a wave of small tech firms going public in the coming months. The *Times* didn't start writing about Cisco in its daily market round-ups until as late as Nov. 8, 1991. By then, Cisco Systems had more than tripled in price from its proper buy point back on Oct. 18, 1990.

The *Wall Street Journal* did a better job than the *Times* in covering Cisco's early run. It included Cisco in 16 articles, based on a search on factiva.com. But in most of those articles, Cisco got no more than a passing mention.

On May 11, 1990, the Dow Jones News Service sent out an 84-word story on Cisco's fiscal third-quarter earnings, up a spectacular 189% to 26 cents a share. (Reuters had covered it in 60 words a day earlier.) But evidently, editors at the *Journal* didn't think this piece of news was worth publishing in the paper the next day. The same thing happened on Aug. 16, 1990, when Cisco announced superb fiscal fourth-quarter results for the three-month period ended in July. And again, three months later.

The *Journal* did catch Cisco's big initial spurt with articles in October and November; but judging by titles such as "Several of Morgan Stanley's New Issues Bombed This Year; Gulf Crisis Blamed" on Oct. 29 and "Technology Stocks Look Bubbly for Now, But January May Be a Rude Awakening" on Dec. 10, the mood was mostly skeptical. The first Cisco feature in the *Journal* arrived on May 16, 1994, nearly four years after the stock's initial breakout to new highs. By then, Cisco had roared ahead as much as 2,400%. The *Journal*'s story highlighted the negative, as can be seen in the lead paragraph:

Call it the great computer networking scare of 1994. After four years of defying gravity, Wall Street darling Cisco Sys-

tems Inc. touched off a selling avalanche Friday that roared
through one of high-tech's hottest markets.

> —From "Cisco Systems, Rivals Receive a Short
> Course on Gravity—After Hot Streak, Computer
> Networking Industry Appears to Be Cooling Off,"
> 1,214 words, *Wall Street Journal*, May 16, 1994

Perhaps investors were scared away from Cisco, when in fact they
should have put it on their watch lists.

The business weeklies didn't do much better. *Fortune* ignored
Cisco until May 20, 1991, when it spared it a paragraph in a "Companies to Watch" story. *Forbes* was quicker to the trigger. In its Nov. 12,
1990, issue, *Forbes* ran its "200 Best Small Companies in America"
and included Cisco. Interestingly, the magazine noted that most of
the data for the list was compiled from William O'Neil + Co. in Los
Angeles, IBD's sister firm!

Meanwhile, IBD kept highlighting and writing about Cisco in its
market round-ups and stock screens because the stock continued to
show unusual increases in earnings and unusual stock-price
strength. It made the daily OTC/Amex round-up more than a dozen
times from Oct. 1 to Dec. 31 that year. On Dec. 17, 1990, IBD ran
"Cisco Systems: Silicon Valley's Hottest Story," which was the first
major feature among the national publications. Sean Silverthorne's
1,009-word piece focused on the startup's clear leadership position
in the fast-growing "inter-networking" market. "The company's
biggest problem, it seems, is keeping growth in control," Silverthorne wrote. He quoted Cisco CEO John Morgridge as saying,
"'We're kind of like a kid that is going from being six years old to
being 25 in a period of two years, and it puts a lot of stress on the
structure.'"

In its weekly feature on computer stocks on Oct. 30, 1990, IBD
published a screen simply called "400 Computer Companies Listed

By Earnings Per Share Rank." Cisco ranked seventh. Its annual profit growth rate over the past five years had been a staggering +262%! No other company on that table could match that growth. Some other fantastic stocks also made the top 25: American Power Conversion (no. 9), Microsoft (no. 11), Novell (no. 15) and Dell Computer (no. 16). In the same screen published on Oct. 1, 1991, Cisco ranked second. Several weeks later on Oct. 30, Cisco roared out of a new base and plowed ahead to all-time highs.

## More Screens Than a Cineplex

Cisco was no fluke. IBD's philosophy on how to present the stock market action has yielded plenty of information on dozens of the biggest stock market winners. They've come in the form of the NYSE and Nasdaq "Stocks In The News" feature; the "Your Weekly Review" screen of stocks with EPS and RS Ratings of 85 or higher; the IBD "Screen Of The Day"; the "Industry Snapshot"; a variety of stock screens in the "Internet & Technology" pages showing the fastest-growing tech firms; the "IBD 100 Index"; the "Daily Stock Analysis" (formerly called the "IBD WebLink"); and the "SmartLink."

From the beginning, IBD has never told readers to "buy this" or "sell that." That's like giving someone a fish every day. The paper's aim has been much bigger: to teach investors *how* to fish for a lifetime.

The trend didn't end in 2003. Consider the table in Figure 2.5.

## Know the Other Side of the Coin

The sun and moon. Love and hate. Work, play. Good buy rules, good sell rules.

IBD has always stressed the last pair, no matter what kind of market that investors face. Why can't most people, and professional money managers, for that matter, beat the market? They haven't

## Featuring The Best Stocks, Not The Biggest

IBD featured emerging stock leaders in 2003 much more frequently and in depth than its peers

| Company | Breakout | At breakout | | | Gain, pivot to peak in 2003 | No. of times featured in articles, 2003 | |
|---|---|---|---|---|---|---|---|
| | | Composite | EPS | RS | | IBD | WSJ |
| Schnitzer Steel | 2/24/03 | n.a. | 98 | 92 | 453% | 32 | 3 |
| eResearch Tech | 2/5/03 | 95 | 80 | 95 | 446 | 31 | 4 |
| Ceradyne | 4/30/03 | n.a. | 74 | 82 | 358 | 26 | 7 |
| NetEase.com | 4/7/03 | 96 | 80 | 99 | 306 | 46 | 6 |
| OmniVision Tech | 3/13/03 | 99 | 80 | 96 | 241 | 50 | 5 |
| Amazon.com | 3/13/03 | 89 | 70 | 94 | 162 | 12* | 37* |
| Coach | 2/25/03 | 97 | 98 | 85 | 144 | 24* | 17* |
| Harman Int'l | 4/15/03 | 92 | 91 | 85 | 134 | 34 | 3 |
| Mobile TeleSys. | 2/28/03 | 98 | 81 | 81 | 116 | 60 | 2 |
| eBay | 1/6/03 | 99 | 97 | 96 | 83 | 35* | 46* |

Note: Article totals exclude WSJ's tables on short interest, New Securities Issues and New Stock Listings as well as IBD's Where The Big Money's Flowing, New Buys of Top Mutual Funds and Your Weekly Review tables. Composite = IBD Composite Rating, EPS = Earnings Per Share Rating, RS = Relative Price Strength Rating

*search for company name, "stock" and "rose" in article; source: factiva.com

### Articles appearing before or just as these stocks began their big rallies

**eResearch Technology (ERES), breakout on 2/5/03**

"The Nasdaq Real Most Active: Nasdaq Gains 0.9% But Logs Third Down Week" (Craig Shaw, markets writer), 9/16/02, IBD

"New Leaders In Groups Making Gains" (Paul Katzeff, mutual funds section), 10/29/02, IBD

"Medical Software Maker eResearch Up Wednesday After Beating Views" (Donna Howell, Internet & Technology section), 2/6/03, IBD

"The Nasdaq Real Most Active: War Tremors Cancel Out Early-Session Rally" (Jonah Keri, markets writer), 2/6/03, IBD

"Small-Stock Focus: Hain Celestial Gains 22% on Earnings Forecast," 2/6/03, WSJ

**NetEase.com (NTES), breakout on 4/7/03**

"Profits Sparking Internet-Stock Gains" (Katzeff), 3/13/03, IBD

"The Nasdaq Real Most Active: Nasdaq Slides 0.9%, But Ends Week With Gain" (Shaw), 4/7/03, IBD

"The Nasdaq Real Most Active: Late Reversal Dampens Big Nasdaq Morning" (Keri), 4/8/03, IBD

"The Big Picture" (Chris Gessel, markets editor), 4/8/03, IBD

"Chinese Internet Companies Spotlight Country's Growth Potential" (Michael Krey, Internet & Technology editor), 4/15/03, IBD

Wall Street Journal - none

**(a)**

**Figure 2.5**   (a) Big stock winners in 2003. (b) Articles by IBD and WSJ that appeared before they began their rallies.

### OmniVision Technologies (OVTI), breakout on 3/13/03

"Tech Rally Lifts Growth Funds In Week" (Dan Moreau, mutual funds section), 2/24/03, IBD

"The Nasdaq Real Most Active: Nasdaq Climbs 1% To Close February With Gains" (Shaw), 3/3/03, IBD

"The Big Picture" (Gessel), 3/7/03, IBD

"The Nasdaq Real Most Active: Trade Spikes As Techs Post Best Day In Months" (Shaw), 3/14/03, IBD

"The Big Picture" (Gessel), 3/17/03, IBD

Wall Street Journal - none

### Coach (COH), breakout on 2/25/03

"The NYSE Real Most Active: Blue Chips Mixed On Lighter Volume," 1/14/03, IBD

"The NYSE Real Most Active: NYSE Stocks Rally, But Volume Shrinks," 1/15/03, IBD

"Kodak, General Dynamics Fall as Doleful News Dents Market," 1/23/03, WSJ

"Small-Stock Focus: Imagistics, Arris, Adtran Gain Amid Broad Rally," 1/29/03, WSJ

"The NYSE Real Most Active: Signs Of Cooperation By Iraq Lift Stocks," 2/26/03, IBD

"A Slow Economy Is Bag Maker's Accessory" (Nancy Gondo, markets writer, The New America section), 4/4/03, IBD

### Harman International Industries (HAR), breakout on 4/15/03)

"Audio Systems Maker Tunes Into Car Market" (Marilyn Alva, The New America section), 1/31/03, IBD

"NYSE Stocks In The News" (Keri), 1/31/03, IBD

"NYSE Stocks In The News: Hi-Fi Products Maker Singing Strong Profit" (Saito-Chung), 2/28/03, IBD

"Shareholder Scorecard: The Best & Worst Performers of the WSJ 1000," 3/10/03, WSJ

"NYSE Stocks In The News: Harman, Chico's Etch Base-On-Base Forms" (Keri), 4/3/03, IBD

"The NYSE Real Most Active," featured 10 times from 2/3/03 to 4/17/03, IBD

### Mobile TeleSystems (MBT), breakout on 2/28/03

"The NYSE Real Most Active: Broad Rally Shoves NYSE Stocks Higher," 1/10/03, IBD

"Use WebLink As Your Investment Tutor" (Ken Shreve, Investors.com content editor), Investors.com corner, 2/6/03, IBD

"The NYSE Real Most Active: Dow, S&P 500 Log 2nd Straight Up Week," 2/24/03, IBD

"Mobile, Vimpel Offer More Chances To Buy," NYSE Stocks In The News, 2/24/03, IBD

"The NYSE Real Most Active: Upward GDP Revision Boosts Stocks Mildly," 3/3/03, IBD

"Russian Market Keeps This Firm Dialing In" (Kirk Shinkle, The New America section), 3/4/03, IBD

Wall Street Journal - none

**(b)**

53

worked hard at perfecting the technique of selling for big profits and small losses. **IBD has always argued that knowing what and when to buy is only half the battle.** Paper profits are only paper profits.

In 1998, IBD ran a series of front-page interviews with O'Neil about the step-by-step process of picking, buying and selling stocks and sound money management.

In the summer of 1999, I met with O'Neil in his office for the first time. O'Neil, then-markets editor Chris Gessel and I sat and talked about putting the "Investor's Corner" back on the front page. But instead of addressing various topics about the market, O'Neil had a plan to make each column concisely discuss one key step in the art of buying and selling growth stocks. I was game. The inaugural column, on Aug. 23, 1999, highlighted the golden rule of investing:

> In the battle for investment survival, you can learn a lot from judo. The first and most important lesson in that martial art is the same for the stock market: damage control.
>
> Judo masters begin not by learning how to throw, but how to fall. They practice this skill until it's as natural as breathing. No matter how many times they're flipped, they can rise to fight again.
>
> Highly successful stock pickers go through similar training: They must learn how to cut their losses short.
>
> This means selling a stock when it's down 7% or 8% from your purchase price. Sounds simple, but many investors have learned the hard way how difficult it is to master the most important rule in investing.
>
> No one wants to sell for a loss. It's an admission that you made a mistake. But if you can set your ego aside, you can take a small loss and still be fit enough, both financially and mentally, to invest the next day. Cutting losses quickly pre-

vents you from suffering a devastating fall that's too steep to recover from.

—From "Rule No. 1: Cut Your Stock Losses Quickly," "Investor's Corner," front page, IBD, Aug. 23, 1999

That wasn't the only time IBD made a big deal about keeping your losses on every stock small. As the mighty bull market of 1982 to 2000 morphed into a horrible bear market, IBD kept hammering the point home. In contrast, some Wall Street analysts told people on cable TV shows to buy tech stocks on the dips. Other financial magazines continued to recommend stocks to buy.

*"Investor's Corner" Columns on the Importance of Cutting Losses*

*Feb. 14, 2000:* Cast Your Ego Aside: Cut Losses Quickly (writer: Ed Carson)

*April 12, 2000:* Bad Market Shows Beauty Of Cutting Losses (Carson)

*May 16, 2000:* Cut Initial Losses Short But Let Winners Ride (Carson)

*June 1, 2000:* Don't Let Big Stock Losses Get Even Bigger (Carson)

*Aug. 8, 2000:* Cut Losses To Preserve Confidence, Capital (David Saito-Chung)

*Oct. 13, 2000:* Cutting Losses Protects You From Bad Market (Christina Wise)

*Oct. 27, 2000:* Taking Small Losses Guards Against Big Hits (Saito-Chung)

*Nov. 2, 2000:* Don't Lose Your Resolve To Cut Initial Losses (Wise)

*Nov. 14, 2000:* Don't Let Small Loss Turn Into Major Casualty (Wise)

**(The Nasdaq fell 39% in 2000; the S&P 500 lost 10%.)**

*Jan. 2, 2001:* Bear Proves Why Cutting Losses Is Rule No. 1 (Saito-Chung)

*Feb. 8, 2001:* Keep Sound Trading Rules In Bear Market (Jonah Keri)

*March 6, 2001:* Cut Your Losses And Leave The Crowd Behind (Keri)

*March 22, 2001:* Use Sound Rules To Avoid Devastating Losses (Keri)

*June 5, 2001:* Even In Bull Market, Cut Your Losses Short (Monika Tjia)

*Aug. 20, 2001:* Cutting Losses Shields You From Bad Times (IBD staff)

*Oct. 29, 2001:* Winning Traders Sell Losers Quickly (Wise)

**(The Nasdaq fell 24% in 2001; the S&P 500 lost 14%.)**

*Jan. 30, 2002:* Always Keep Your Losses Small (Keri)

*June 5, 2002:* Cutting Losses Preserves Confidence And Capital (Craig Shaw)

*July 2, 2002:* In Any Market, Employ A Sound Win-Loss Ratio (Keri)

*Oct. 1, 2002:* Limiting Losses To 8% Still No. 1 Investing Rule (Shaw)

*Jan. 10, 2003:* When To Sell For Tinier Losses (Saito-Chung)

*April 17, 2003:* Always Cut Losses Short To Preserve Your Confidence (Keri)

*Aug. 18, 2003:* Cutting Losses Remains No. 1 Rule Even In A Rapidly Rising Market (Keri)

*Sept. 18, 2003:* Apply Investing's No. 1 Rule On Every Stock You Buy (Saito-Chung)

*Dec. 30, 2003:* Even In A Strong Market, Don't Forget The Golden
   Rule (Nancy Gondo)

**(The Nasdaq fell 43% from Jan. 1, 2002, to its low on Oct. 10,
   2002; the S&P 500 lost 33%.)**

## Cut Your Losses!

If all investors had followed this rule in 2000, 2001 and 2002, would
the bear market have been less painful? Definitely yes.

O'Neil always cuts his losses short. At an IBD seminar in 2002, he
told the crowd of roughly 300 that he often sells losing stocks faster
when he spots poor action by the stock. His average loss per stock
tends to be around 5%, not 7% to 8%.

When O'Neil began as a broker in Los Angeles in 1958, there
were 17 regional firms that were members of the New York Stock
Exchange. Many years later his brokerage was still surviving, but
many of the 17 regional LA brokerage firms were not, he says. Why?
O'Neil and the paper's followers cut losses at 7%. "Many of these original 17 firms would ride a big position down 70% or 80%," O'Neil said
in a March 1991 interview. "Even in their firm accounts. I know a couple of them took some huge positions down from $90 a share to $5 or
$10. You make one mistake like that, and that's it. I always cut all of
my losses at 7% or 8%. I have never gotten into a jam." Many of these
firms had to merge with stronger ones.

After the "Investor's Corner" returned to the front page in August
1999, the column also ran hundreds of articles explaining how to use
charts to find the right time to sell a stock and lock in profits—that is,
when it's reached a peak and is beginning a big decline. One column
was devoted to one sell rule, and the "Investor's Corner" ran series of
articles on these rules. (The column was later moved to the front page
of the paper's second section.)

## One More Look At All The Major Sell Rules

Investor's Corner, July 23, 2001

If you have read this column since June 14, nice going. You just covered 25 major sell rules.

Of course, knowing them is one thing. Pulling them out of your quiver and firing them at the right moment in the market is another.

It takes time and practice to master each one. You don't need a Ph.D.—that is, unless perhaps it's the kind that value fund manager Mario Gabelli has said he looks for: Poor, Hungry and a Deep desire to succeed.

You may want to clip this column and tape it on the wall or a place where you can quickly refer to it. Review these rules to preserve your capital and maximize your gains.

1. **Cut your losses short.** Sell when a stock falls 7% to 8% below your buy price. You bought it thinking it would go up, didn't you?
2. **Sell into a climax run.** A 25% to 50% gain in a week or two? After the stock's already doubled, tripled in price? Great! No, too great! No stock goes vertical for long.
3. **New highs on low volume.** Buying is going flat, especially if past highs came on healthy trade.
4. **Stock slices through trend line.** Remember to draw them over a period of at least four to six months.
5. **Leaders in the sector crack.** Stocks tend to move in packs. When the top performers tumble, the whole sector could be in trouble.
6. **Institutions sell hard.** When the major averages post four or five distribution days within a week or two, the market is in great danger. Fund managers are rushing for the exits.

7. **Stock declines on the heaviest volume since its breakout.** A hint that institutions are getting out. It may lack strength for more gains.

8. **High-volume churn.** Lots of trading activity, little price progress.

9. **Earnings growth slows.** Two quarters of slower growth, or a 66% deceleration, can spell doom.

10. **Late-stage base.** Three or four bases are usually the limit. Five are rare.

11. **Stock rebounds in lighter trade after sharp sell-offs.** Proof of why it's worthwhile to study a daily chart for price and volume clues.

12. **CEO appears on magazine cover.** By then the public knows the stock too well. What works in the market isn't necessarily obvious.

13. **Excessive stock splits.** When it happens, optimism runs rampant.

14. **Stock fails to stay above its 50-day moving average.** Especially bad if down days occur on heavy trade.

15. **Stock stages its biggest price gain of the rally.** Often coincides with a climax run.

16. **Breaks through an upper channel line.** Rally gets out of control.

17. **Fails to follow through after breakout.** The initial thrust higher tends to last more than a day. If it doesn't, the breakout will likely fail.

18. **Head-and-shoulders pattern.** A late sell signal. Try to spot others first.

19. **Closes excessively above the 50-day.** Enthusiasm reaches a boil.

20. **Relative Strength line fails to reach new high ground at breakout.** Use investors.com charts to spot this.

21. **Exhaustion gap.** A spectacular way to end a rally.

22, 23. **Breaks out from sloppy base or on below-average volume.** Such action is failure-prone.

24. **P-E ratio rises 121% since breakout.** When this occurs, look for other key sell signals.

25. **Sell your laggards, force-feed your winners.** You want to reap the biggest possible gains, right? Underperformers are dead weight.

## Timing the Market

What does this phrase exactly mean? If you do it right, you buy stocks around the market's bottom and sell them at or around the top.

The mainstream media, the mutual fund industry's PR machine, elite academics and many financial planners have always warned that you shouldn't time the market. Why? You simply can't, they say.

> Roger Ibbotson, a Yale University professor who heads the Chicago investment consulting firm bearing his name, concedes there are often imbalances in the market that investors could benefit from responding to in the short term—such as getting out of technology stocks in early 2000. But he says most investors shouldn't attempt to make such calls.
>
> "Maybe a hedge fund might be able to do this sort of thing and make some money, but I think it's a more dangerous policy for individuals," Mr. Ibbotson says. **"Most individuals and even most institutional investors shouldn't get involved in the markets this way."** (emphasis added)
>
> —Tom Lauricella, "Those Dirty Words: Market Timing,"
> *Wall Street Journal*, Aug. 27, 2003

Hogwash!

Those who invest in mutual funds don't have to time the market. Holding a good diversified stock fund through 10 or 15 years' worth of bull and bear market cycles or longer is smart. But those who buy and sell stocks have greater risk for two reasons. First, stocks fall harder than the major indexes, and second, roughly three out of four stocks follow the market's general direction. So in a bear market, three out of every four stocks in the average portfolio are going south. That's why fleeing into cash is better than letting stock holdings slide.

Individuals *should* learn to time the market. They hold smaller positions than the growth fund manager who owns $900 million worth of stock. So individuals can get into the market and out of the market quickly, sometimes within seconds.

Individuals *can* time the market. Why? Because it's not that hard. It just takes a pair of eyes, the willingness to observe market action objectively, practice and a dose of experience. IBD's "Big Picture" column, which began on Sept. 15, 1998, shows millions of readers how it's done.

Let's go back in time to the spring of 2000. The Nasdaq composite had scored five straight years of double-digit percentage gains. It had also sprinted from 2,632 on Oct. 18, 1999, to 4,904 on March 6, 2000—up 86% in less than five months! But the market rally showed signs of overheating. On March 7, the Nasdaq composite began the day higher. But it reversed course and closed the day down 57.01 points, or 1.2%, to 4,847.84. Volume rose to 2.14 billion shares. This combination of a decline in a major index on higher volume than the previous session is called a *distribution*.

Why should you care? Institutional investors sold stocks hard. They were more eager to dump shares than to accumulate them. It's the market's way of saying *Auf wiedersehen* to stocks and hello to profits. Figure 2.6 shows what that day looked like in IBD the next day.

Next to the chart was the "Big Picture" column. "The Nasdaq suffered its first loss in heavier volume since late January (3). Even down

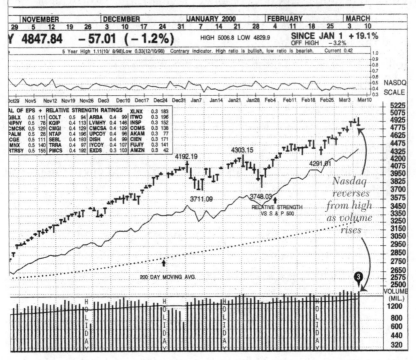

# Spotting The Market Top

## GENERAL MARKET & SECTORS

*A view of the Nasdaq composite index from the "General Market & Sectors" page in IBD, March 8, 2000. The page also ran the daily charts of the S&P 500 and the Dow Jones Industrial Average.*

**Figure 2.6**  The Nasdaq in March 2000.

volume managed to beat up volume, another rarity (4)," the column wrote.

Sure, the Nasdaq is stuffed with techs. So it's more prone to big price swings. Yet the broader market had an even worse day! The S&P 500 large-cap benchmark dropped 2.6%, and the Dow industrial average skidded 3.7% lower. Volume on the NYSE shot up 28%! Practically every portfolio that day took a bruising.

Now, who should care about a day like that? Every investor should! When you have three or more of these distribution days over a period of just one to two weeks, it's like the *Titanic*'s striking an iceberg. The market doesn't fall to the bottom of the ocean right away. It takes time. But the flurry of distributions shows that a major shift in the market is taking place. The balance of demand and supply in the market has tilted from the former to the latter. The size of the sellers' orders begins to exceed how much the buyers want. A bear market is born.

On March 8, the day after that first distribution, the Nasdaq rebounded 1%, a nice gain. But volume declined 7% from the prior day. In just these two days of action, the careful investor would have discovered that enthusiasm for buying stocks was weaker than enthusiasm for selling them. Still, it takes three or more distributions in a short span to send the signal to sell, get off margin, and start locking in profits.

Distribution day no. 2 came on March 10. The Nasdaq reached as high as 5,132.50, but it sold off toward the end of the day to end up just 1.76 points at 5,048.62. Volume fell slightly, but it was still heavy. Although the Nasdaq didn't decline, it was still an unpleasant reversal. The "Big Picture" noted this churn, another form of distribution, and warned: "A short- to intermediate-term correction wouldn't be unwarranted. After a volatile January, the tech-heavy Nasdaq has rumbled 28% higher in less than six weeks. Behind that gain are some massive moves in individual stocks."

The column also noted that most of the leading stocks in the tech sectors looked fine, except for the biotechs. Well, two sessions later, these stocks got crushed. On March 14, the Nasdaq fell 200.60 points, or 4.1%, to 4,706.63. Turnover ballooned 17% to 1.98 billion shares:

A budding tech correction took a turn for the worse Tuesday after President Clinton sparked a sell-off in genomic stocks. He and Prime Minister Tony Blair called for free access to the raw data generated by biotech companies mapping the human genome. But the two leaders stressed that inventions based on the information should be protected by law.

Investors focused on the first part of their joint statement and dumped biotechs of all types with a vengeance. The group, which had been faltering the past week, tumbled 13.6%, the biggest loser for the day.

—"The Big Picture," March 15, 2000, IBD

Including this sell-off, the market had now suffered three distribution days in just six sessions. The Nasdaq's mighty rally had just hit an iceberg. Several paragraphs later in the column, the "Big Picture" sounded the alarm:

Whether you try to ride out the market or take some profits, it's prudent to ease off margin. There's no sense in watching massive gains of the past few months vanish under the weight of an overleveraged portfolio.

—"The Big Picture," March 15, 2000, IBD

On March 15, the Nasdaq lopped off another 124 points, or 2.6%, to 4582.62. This time, trading slowed down by a notch. Yet the damage was already done.

It was a weird session. The S&P 500 jumped up 2.4%, and the Dow sprang back up 3.3% as the NYSE volume soared. Chris Gessel, IBD's "Big Picture" columnist at the time, didn't pull any punches. "The dogs of the market bounded like happy puppies Wednesday as money poured out of technology stocks for a third straight session," he wrote.

The heavy selling by professional investors continued. The Nasdaq suffered three distribution days in a row on March 28, 29 and 30. It fell 10.1% over the span, and volume was higher than the previous session. So in less than four weeks, the market logged five distribution days and one day of churning. The institutions as a whole weren't grabbing shares any more. They were dumping them and racing for the exits.

A top was in the making.

If you think all this fuss about the daily price-and-volume action is nonsense, consider what the market did in the next month, which is shown in Figure 2.7.

In the week ended April 14, the Nasdaq melted 25%. That's right—the leading index lost one-fourth of its market value! It was the

## Spotting The Market Top - Part II

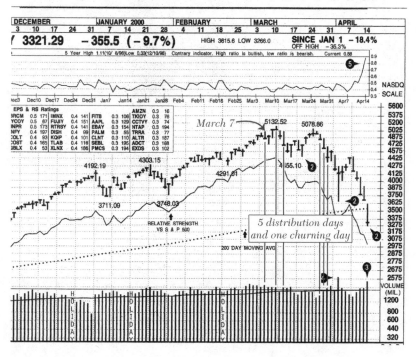

*A view of the Nasdaq after its 25% plunge from April 10 to 14, from the General Market & Sectors page in IBD, April 17, 2000.*

**Figure 2.7** The Nasdaq in April 2000.

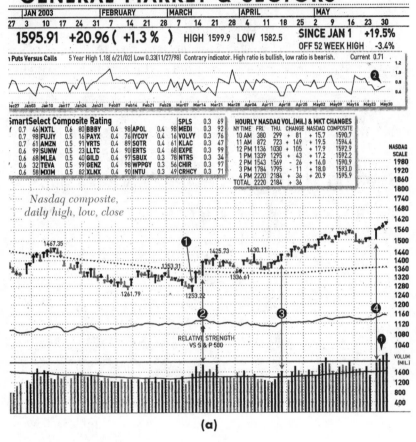

**Figure 2.8** (a and b)   The Nasdaq from March to May 2003.

worst weekly drop for the index ever, eclipsing October 1987's infamous 19% plunge. Everyone knows what happened after that. The Nasdaq went on to fall 78%, the S&P 500 51%. Cisco fell harder. It lost as much as 90%. Sun Microsystems dropped 96%. Many dot-com stocks, whose business models were as flimsy as the cocktail napkins they were initially written upon, fell to pennies a share or got delisted. Only after the stock market topped did the public come to find out

**1** After falling 18% from December 2002, the Nasdaq begins a new rally attempt on March 12, 2003.

**2** The Nasdaq soars 3.9% on heavier volume on March 17, a strong follow-through on the fourth day of the new rally attempt. The volume was well above its 50-day average. The "Big Picture" column wrote in the next day's paper:

*"A follow-through is not a green light to buy any old stock with abandon. It doesn't mean you should rush out on margin and make an all-or-nothing bet on the Nasdaq 100 or some other exchange-traded fund.*

*"A follow-through tells disciplined growth investors the market's trend has turned up. Armed with that knowledge, you can carefully buy fundamentally strong stocks breaking out of sound price bases. Don't chase stocks that are far extended past their proper buy points. Be ready to cut any loss quickly if the market or a stock moves against you.*

*"As more stocks break out successfully, both in your portfolio and in the market at large, you can become more aggressive."*

**3** The Nasdaq gains 2.2% on higher volume on April 17, ahead of the Easter holiday. The next day's "Big Picture" on the front page noted the market's new bullish tone again:

*"By the close, Nasdaq volume was up almost 6% to 1.62 billion shares. In contrast, turnover on the NYSE paled 9%. That's not surprising, as traders left ahead of the three-day Easter holiday. What's more meaningful is the boost in Nasdaq turnover, yet another signal that institutions are seriously building new positions in the market.*

*"The best part of the day's action? Investors continued to grab shares of the leading stocks. What ultimately should give you confidence to look for new breakouts is the sight of strong gains among the market's current leaders."*

**4** The Nasdaq surges again on May 27, this time rising 3.1% as volume swells. The May 28 "Big Picture" column's "Market Pulse" table notes these leading stocks up in volume: Usana Health, Genentech, NetEase.com, Amazon.com, Yahoo, Sohu.com and Shuffle Master.

**(b)**

about the corporate accounting scandals. Enron and WorldCom went bankrupt. CFOs got handcuffed.

Yet as the market showed back in March 2000, investors knew that the wild bidding up of tech stocks had to end.

Market tops can be spotted because they all look more or less the same. They can be spotted because human nature hasn't changed. Stocks peak when investor greed and love for stocks are at peak levels.

Countless IBD readers benefited from this objective, scientific analysis of the market's action. They've also benefited from IBD's identifying the market's bottom in late 2002 to early 2003. (See Figure 2.8.)

## Picking the Winners Better Than Most Pros

Some readers understood IBD's wisdom and profited handsomely.

Frances Jones, a dentist in Texas, made a habit of scanning the stock tables every day. After a while, as she went through the stock tables, Jones noticed that IBD made a habit of boldfacing Cisco Systems. She told her twin sister, Florence Rutherford, about it.

"She watched the new-highs list, and it kept popping up," Jones said in an April 4, 2002, feature in IBD's "The Smart Investor" page. "She also read the boldfaced stocks in the tables, and Cisco would be in bold every day."

Jones and Rutherford began buying shares in August 1992. They added shares over the years when Cisco broke out of a new base. Then they held it. And held it. Cisco, whose EPS Rating remained in the high 90s during the 1990s, vaulted more than 70,000% from its original buy point to its 2000 split-adjusted high of 82. Undo the splits, and the stock rose from its pivot, or the right entry point to start buying shares, of $25 per share to around $17,500!

In early 2000, the twins went up to O'Neil at an IBD seminar in Los Angeles and asked him whether Cisco had topped. O'Neil told the two energetic Texans to review their sell rules—such as climax runs, new highs on low volume, and breakdowns through the 50-day moving average on huge volume followed by a weak recovery. The twins studied their rules again. Cisco's action triggered these and other sell rules. So they began to sell. By August 2000, they had sold the last of their Cisco shares. The pair had bagged tremendous gains in a single stock. By using charts and the paper, Jones and Rutherford latched on to many other great winners during the 1990s. Microsoft, Dell, America Online,

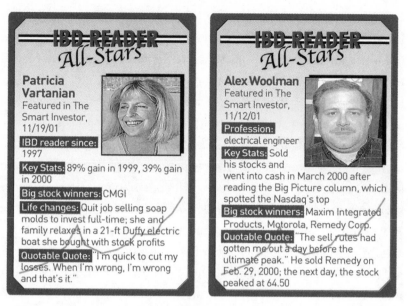

**IBD READER**
*All-Stars*

**Patricia Vartanian**
Featured in The Smart Investor, 11/19/01
IBD reader since: 1997
Key Stats: 89% gain in 1999, 39% gain in 2000
Big stock winners: CMGI
Life changes: Quit job selling soap molds to invest full-time; she and family relaxes in a 21-ft Duffy electric boat she bought with stock profits
Quotable Quote: "I'm quick to cut my losses. When I'm wrong, I'm wrong and that's it."

**IBD READER**
*All-Stars*

**Alex Woolman**
Featured in The Smart Investor, 11/12/01
Profession: electrical engineer
Key Stats: Sold his stocks and went into cash in March 2000 after reading the Big Picture column, which spotted the Nasdaq's top
Big stock winners: Maxim Integrated Products, Motorola, Remedy Corp.
Quotable Quote: "The sell rules had gotten me out a day before the ultimate peak." He sold Remedy on Feb. 29, 2000; the next day, the stock peaked at 64.50

**Figure 2.9** Alex Woolman and Patricia Vartanian, IBD Reader All Stars.

Qualcomm, Yahoo—you name it, they had it. Their accountants calculated that their personal accounts grew at a 57% annual compounded rate of return from 1988 to 1999. Few money managers can match that.

"We didn't take it all off the top, but we took a lot and kept a lot of what we had," Rutherford said. "When Cisco had been struggling around the 50-day moving average line in 2000, it made us go to the seminars and reread O'Neil's books and really find out how to sell. We needed more info on how to sell. I believe those charts really show you that."

Selling a great stock like Cisco wasn't easy.

Rutherford's friends were aghast when they heard she and her twin sister had unloaded the stock.

With Cisco, "It was like selling a member of your family," Rutherford said. "But you have to put the market first and watch what it is doing every day. This is so, so important. The market's action told everyone to get out in 2000."

The twins were glad they did. No stock, even Cisco, could defy the selling avalanche that followed the Nasdaq's peak. The stock tried to form a late-stage base from March to September 2000, but it failed to finish the base, which is another key sell signal. In the meantime, the Nasdaq and S&P 500 suffered another storm of distribution days in early September soon after the Labor Day weekend. In the week ended Sept. 15, 2000, Cisco closed below its 200-day moving average on the heaviest weekly trade in three months. The stock continued to sell off hard the next five weeks. Cisco's rebound attempts were smaller in price compared to the declines and came on lower volume. It was time to unload shares and take profits.

From March 2000 to October 2002, the stock fell 90% to as low as 8.12 as the Internet generation experienced one of the worst bear markets in the history of humankind. Rutherford says she feels almost guilty about doing so well because so many people she knew had ridden Cisco and other tech wonders all the way down to their 2002 lows.

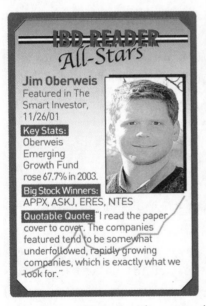

**Figure 2.10** Jim Oberweis and Jim Sugano, IBD Reader All Stars.

The big gains have helped Rutherford and Jones change their lives and hopefully the lives of others for the better. Rutherford contributed to the University of Texas medical school's cardiology division, and she helped a local museum of medical science get off the ground. She entertains friends and family at a second home in Colorado. The twins have also taken Jones' son on trips around the world, including Switzerland, France and Italy. "It's been very educational for him," Rutherford said.

## A Continuous Learning Process

Alas, not all readers follow the IBD system. A recent reader survey showed that 10.8% of respondents always follow CAN SLIM rules, while 38% follow them most times. More than half follow the rules sometimes or never.

During the 2000–02 bear market, even if investors had known and followed only the 7% stop-loss rule, they would have saved a lot of money.

Investing is a frustrating job. Members of the IBD markets team have received nasty letters and e-mails from a few disgruntled readers. In most cases, though, their difficulties are due to a lack of complete understanding about all the rules on choosing stocks and reading charts.

"Thanks to you and your fellow markets writers, I've lost quite a lot of money!"

One man greeted me this way at an IBD seminar on April 19, 2004 . He wasn't angry, though. The man, a veteran rocket scientist, talked in a soft, gentle voice and smiled as he greeted me. I had first met him at a seminar in December 2003 at the Hyatt Regency Hotel in downtown Los Angeles. We had a cordial conversation, and he told me with a difficult smile he had lost a million bucks during the bear market.

I wanted to know just what was going wrong. So we went outside the seminar room to the banquet room lobby, where several notebook PCs were hooked up to some wide-screen plasma TVs showing Daily Graphs.

He showed me his list of a dozen stocks he owned, when he bought them, at what price, and how much up or down he was. We punched in the tickers of a few of his key holdings and looked at the daily charts of the stocks on the large screen. As we discussed where the pivot point was—the proper price to buy shares as a stock rushes out of a bullish chart pattern, such as the cup with handle—the man started nodding his head. He suddenly grew quiet upon his discovery. He realized he had been buying good stocks, stocks with earnings and revenue growth that put most of the members of the Dow Jones industrial average to shame. Yet he had been buying them *way too late* into the rally. A great stock can go up 20% or 40% in just a month or two, then fall 10%, 20% or more. That's natural. No stock goes straight up. That's why you need to buy right. If you don't, you'll be forced to cut your losses by 7%, and you'll be knocked out of a stock during what is otherwise a normal mild correction! Many IBD readers who don't understand or follow all the rules often get cut up by the temporary sell-off because they buy stocks way too extended in price, then follow the 7%–8% loss-cutting rule.

We looked at another chart; he now saw he had bought the stock at $45 when the pivot point was $35. His purchase price was nearly 29% higher than where he should have bought it! I turned away from the screen and looked at him to see if he was agreeing with my analysis. He nodded again. You could tell by the look in his eyes that he was going through a fundamental change in how he would look at charts and how he would buy a stock. He walked briskly back into the seminar room. It's likely that over time, he'll make back those losses by finding the next Home Depots and Microsofts of the market.

# Back to Wal-Mart

The *LA Times'* Pulitzer-winning three-part Wal-Mart feature that ran from Nov. 23 to 25, 2003, was awesome. That is to say, it was awesome in terms of word count (9,579 words plus three sidebars), in its analysis of how much pricing power the world's largest retailer wields, and in that the articles may have played a role in Inglewood's decision to block a new Wal-Mart in that neighborhood of Los Angeles.

The *LA Times* did a great job of informing the public. But did the article make readers any money? On Nov. 25, 2003, the stock closed at 56.04. As of July 26, Wal-Mart closed at 52.65, down 6%.

IBD began covering Wal-Mart in earnest in May 1984, only a month after the paper's debut. The stock had already bolted 2,100% after breaking out of a 17-month double-bottom base. But the Arkansas-based retailer kept growing its profits and sales and kept getting more efficient. Its stock rested for nearly two years after posting an all-time high of 46.63 in July 1983. Then on May 10, 1985, Wal-Mart surged out of a base-on-top-of-a-base, which itself was on top of yet another base structure. It gapped up seven-eighths of a point to 49¼ on sharply higher volume. The stock raced up 253% over the next 27 months. Through March 1993, it ran up 1,023%.

IBD was there. In the May 10, 1985, issue, Wal-Mart's chart appeared on the "NYSE Stocks In The News" page, second from the bottom. It had a 98 EPS Rating and a 68 RS Rating. With 140 million shares, it was big, but not that big. The stock's Relative Strength line was near new high ground—another sign of outstanding strength. In the stock tables, Wal-Mart was also boldfaced because it had hit a 52-week high the day before.

IBD's first big feature on Wal-Mart came on July 24, 1984—10 months before its breakout. Underneath the headline "Wal-Mart Sees Sharp Sales Gains Even In Slow Economy," IBD ran a company Datagraph that covered half the page. Among other things, it showed that earnings per share had risen 38%, 36%, 54%, 43%, 67%, 63%, 48% and 55% from year-ago levels in the prior eight quarters. Sales gains were equally as huge. The Datagraph also showed that two mutual funds had recently built new positions in the stock.

So, as an individual investor, wouldn't you rather read a paper that identified the stock in the infancy of its long, amazing growth spurt, helping increase the standard of living for billions, gave and explained the proper sell rules to lock in those gains, and continued to put the spotlight on new emerging champions of retailing?

Hey, it's America. Everyone has freedom to choose.

Figures 2.11 through 2.18 show eight of the market's elite winners of 2003.

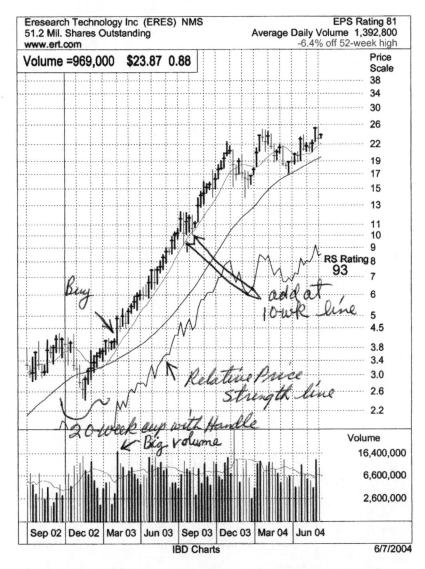

Eresearch Technology Inc (ERES) NMS
51.2 Mil. Shares Outstanding
www.ert.com
EPS Rating 81
Average Daily Volume 1,392,800
-6.4% off 52-week high

Volume =969,000  $23.87  0.88

**Figure 2.11  ERES.** *A Runaway Winner* in 2003: EResearch Technology's pivot point was 18.60 (not around 3.90 as seen on this chart) when the stock broke out of a cup-with-handle base on Feb. 5, 2003. Since then, the stock has had a 2-for-1 split and two 3-for-2 splits. As Bill O'Neil notes on the chart, investors could have added shares to their position as the stock pulled back to its 10-week moving average in July and August 2003. This weekly chart can be seen at www.investors.com.

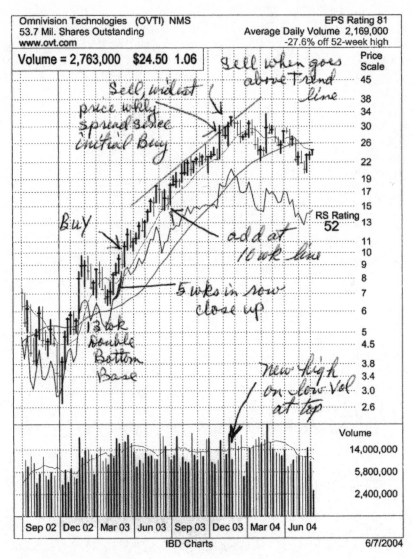

**Figure 2.12 OVTI**. *Say Cheese:* In this weekly chart, available at www.investors.com, O'Neil points out the pivot point, or the exact time to buy, for OmniVision Technologies, one of the biggest winners in 2003. The maker of image sensors for digital cameras and camera-enabled cell phones sported a 99 IBD Composite Rating, an 80 Earnings Per Share Rating, a 96 for Relative Price Strength, and an A- Accumulation/Distribution Rating when it broke out of a 13-week double-bottom base on March 13, 2003.

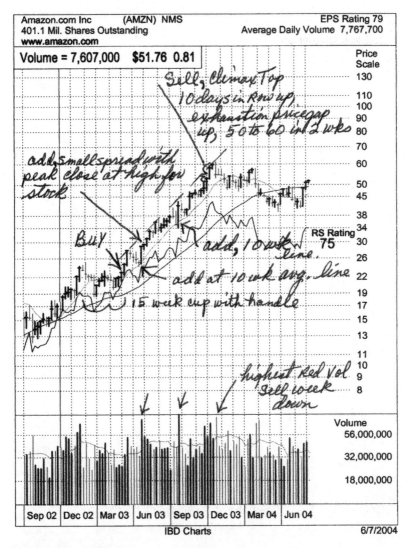

**Figure 2.13  AMAZON.** *Emerging from the Bear Jungle:* Amazon.com made a huge run in 2003 as the online retailer scored profits in the last half of 2002 and strong growth in early 2003. It took off on March 13, 2003, just two days before the stock market staged a big follow-through to signal a new bull run. O'Neil shows on this chart where to add shares to an initial position and where to sell to lock in gains. Internet stocks helped lead the bull market in 2003. When Amazon.com broke out, its Industry Group Relative Strength Rating was an A+.

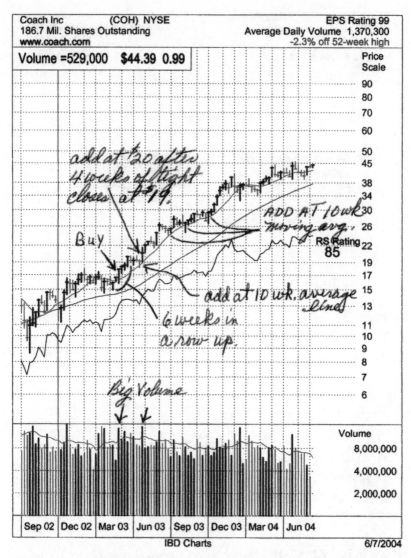

**Figure 2.14   COACH.** *Chic:* Since its market debut in October 2000, luxury handbag and accessories maker Coach has been a rising star among retail stocks. Notice the surges in volume as the stock broke out to new highs in March and April 2003. IBD has featured the company five times in "The New America" from August 2001 through September 2003.

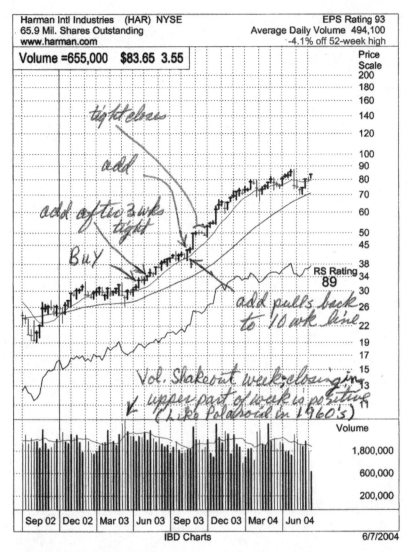

**Figure 2.15 HAR.** *The Sweet Sound of Profits:* Harman International
Industries makes high-end audio equipment and navigation systems for luxury
cars. Earnings grew 114%, 52% and 105% in the three quarters before its breakout to all-time highs on April 16, 2003. Harman was featured 10 times in "The
NYSE Real Most Active" column in IBD from Feb. 3 to April 17, 2003. This chart
includes a 2-for-1 split in December 2003, so the pivot point was actually 64.50.
That might seem "expensive" to those who prefer only to "buy low, sell high."

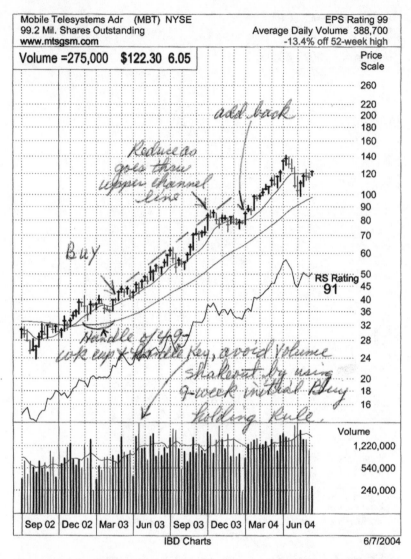

**Figure 2.16 MBT.** *From Russia with Love:* New bull markets tend to feature new leaders, such as Mobile TeleSystems, Russia's no. 1 cell phone service provider. On the chart, O'Neil points out that a high-volume decline midway through the stock's run doesn't necessarily translate into a sell signal. Only part of the huge 49-week cup-with-handle pattern is shown on this chart. Notice how the Relative Strength line (above volume bars in chart) has also driven to new high ground as the stock made its big upward move, a sign of strength.

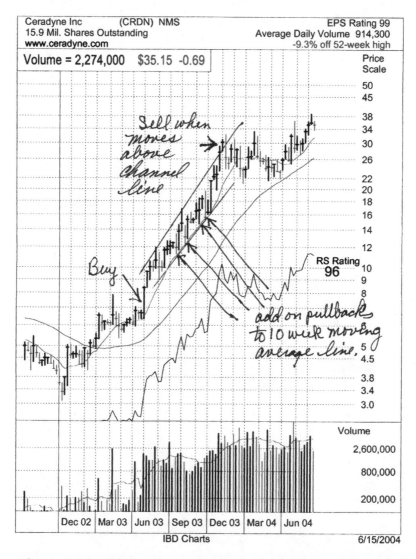

**Figure 2.17  CRDN.** *New Winners Aren't Household Names:* Ceradyne, which makes lightweight body armor for the military, was practically bulletproof during its rally in 2003. The stock split its shares 3-for-2 in April 2004, so the real buy point came at 10.67, not around 7 as seen on this weekly IBD chart. Notice in the 11-week base how the price action is tight and the volume is tame on all four down weeks within the base. O'Neil points out on this chart that an excessive move upward can trigger a sell signal to capture most of the gains.

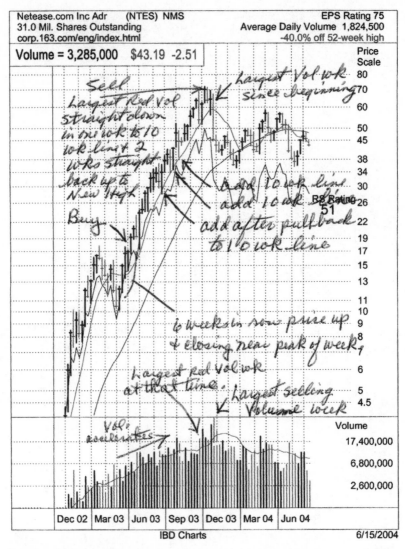

**Figure 2.18  NTES.** *The Year of New Internet Leaders:* NetEase.com was one of the biggest winners in 2003. The provider of wireless Internet content in China surged 304% after breaking out of an 11-week cup-shaped base on April 7, 2003. At the time, revenue had soared 419%, 637%, 941%, 815% and 392% from year-ago levels in the prior five quarters. It also moved firmly into the black in the fourth quarter of 2002. O'Neil notes the first sell signal came in the week ended Sept. 26, 2003, as the stock dropped hard on the biggest weekly volume in a down week. Five weeks later, NetEase.com staged an even deeper sell-off, another timely signal to sell and lock in profits.

# CHAPTER 3

# Lessons for All Entrepreneurs

It's what you learn after you know it all that counts.
> —John Wooden, former basketball coach
> who led UCLA's men's basketball team
> to 10 championships, 1964–75

It is no use saying, "We are doing our best." You have got to succeed in doing what is necessary.
> — Winston Churchill, former British prime minister

Every day gives you another chance.
> — Common saying

There are no secrets to success. It is the result of preparation, hard work and learning from failure.
> — Colin Powell, U.S. secretary of state

Bill O'Neil's office is only 15 steps from the newsroom. The door is often open. O'Neil has said he's deliberately gone with this layout so that people can freely come in and share a thought, a plan, or a question.

In reality, it doesn't really work that way.

O'Neil is constantly on the go. In the morning, unless a meeting or event is scheduled, you won't see him at the office. From 6:15 a.m., he's often at home, making phone calls, reading, writing and watching the market.

On most afternoons, O'Neil will be at the company, but he's rarely sitting behind his desk. He's got to go to a lot of meetings across different ventures (IBD and the printing factory on floor 1, the institutional research firm, brokerage and Daily Graphs on floor 2). He's famous for filling up yellow legal pad after yellow legal pad with notes. He walks quietly but quickly through the hallways. In the 1960s, when the market would turn and rally higher, O'Neil would fire orders at the traders so fast that someone came up with a nickname for him: "The Bullet."

So the most likely place you'll bump into him for a quick chat is in the hallway, the IBD newsroom, or even the men's restroom:

"Have you been making any money in the market?" (O'Neil in December 2003)

"Yes, it's been a great year for me." (IBD staffer)

"So you're living proof that the IBD system works!" (O'Neil, chuckling)

When O'Neil goes to a meeting, he goes in prepared. He has bullet points on his notepad to make sure he covers key points. When someone talks with O'Neil about the business or a new project, he or she must be crystal clear. If not, O'Neil fires back, "What do you mean?" and looks at you as if you had squeezed mustard onto ice cream and began eating.

One day, I asked O'Neil if I could write a chapter in this book on what mistakes, blunders and bonehead errors the paper has made and what lessons it's learned in the newspaper business. O'Neil agreed instantly. No cringe this time. When it comes to learning from one's mistakes and striving to improve, O'Neil is perhaps public advocate numero uno.

"Bill has in a remarkable way been financially successful," said Jessica Jensen, a former consultant at Boston Consulting Group who joined IBD as senior vice president for new product development in April 2004. "But his capacity to accept mistakes and embrace change is truly remarkable."

"In my consulting days, I've met a few Fortune 500 executives, and they are arrogant, defensive, stagnant . . . all the adjectives one can use to describe the word 'immovable,' " Jensen added. "Bill certainly can be stubborn, but some of the strategic changes that have been made [recently] have been truly amazing."

If you blurt out an idea without previously thinking a lot about it, O'Neil will likely shoot it down fast because it's usually one that's riddled with holes, says Kathy Sherman, who's worked for O'Neil for more than 20 years. But "he rarely disagrees if you've done your homework," she said. "He's immovable if you can't prove it to him with facts and data. I would say he's committed to the deepest levels of thinking. He's an analyst to the umpteenth degree."

Whatever the case, O'Neil believes that innate intelligence or natural talent is not enough to gain success. If it were, then why aren't more people successful? Hard work, learning from one's mistakes and making changes for the better must also go into the mix. (Sometimes a little mustard can help too.)

O'Neil was happy to share, to a degree, the paper's mistakes so that future entrepreneurs can benefit from them. Below are a few of the lessons O'Neil and crew have learned during their 20-year voyage.

*If you're starting a new business, first estimate your costs . . . then double them!* The mammoth start-up costs of a national newspaper or magazine make it tough to survive. *USA Today*, which launched in

September 1982, didn't turn a profit until 1993. O'Neil knew that *Sports Illustrated* and other famous publications took many years of losses before turning into the black.

And no wonder. If you're launching a paper in, say, Belgium or Jamaica, your delivery costs are surely going to be less than if you tried to do the same in the 50 states of America. Belgium doesn't have as many cities, towns and villages. It also doesn't have Alaska or Hawaii.

The newspaper business may not be as hard as trying to grow roses between the cement cracks in a parking lot. But imagine trying to deliver a product to every city and town across the U.S. You must send it by plane, then by truck, and finally by hand. Those costs add up. Still, O'Neil felt he had several advantages from the start. He already had printing presses and a database to offer IBD's unique stock tables. He told the media that he had 90% of the ingredients to produce a paper. All he had to do, O'Neil thought, was hire an editorial and marketing staff and spend on advertising.

The personnel costs were in line with expectations, O'Neil says. The curveball came in the form of rapidly rising marketing expenses.

TV ad rates rose faster than the rate of TV viewer growth. At first, it cost roughly $150 to obtain a new subscriber through TV ads. But over the years, that figure grew to nearly $700 per new subscriber— way beyond the price of a one-year subscription to the paper. If you pay out more than what you take in, you're standing on a sinking business. Considering that a one-year subscription cost $84 in the beginning, you can't possibly break even. You've got labor, production, legal and other costs as well. Oh, and don't forget direct advertising, which according to O'Neil came out to roughly $350 per new subscriber.

"The efficiency of obtaining a new subscriber got less and less. At one point, we were advertising every day on cable TV. We were also advertising on network TV, but it was very expensive. And in fact although viewership on the TV networks decreased, ad rates rose. It got to the point where it didn't make any sense," O'Neil said.

Over the 1980s and 1990s, cable TV viewership rose. That's good. A bigger audience raised the chances of new subscribers. But over that same period, advertising rates on cable TV grew at a sharper rate. O'Neil estimates they rose two to three times faster than viewership growth. That's bad.

From the late 1990s, O'Neil decided to cut down on TV ad spending. Thanks to the Internet, IBD has more choices to spread its message. IBD has also finally realized the importance of forming partnerships with leaders in the investing industry, since it can be a low-cost way to get new subscribers. In 2003 and 2004, O'Neil conducted Web casts on Ameritrade for its active-trader customers, explaining the paper's strategies on selecting, buying and selling stocks, and how to spot market tops and bottoms. Ameritrade users can click on a link on ameritrade.com to get not just two free weeks to IBD—either the paper or electronic version— but four weeks.

IBD has also shared its educational content with Yahoo.com, the American Association of Individual Investors, the Money Show, the Online Trading Expo and *Money Matters*, a nationally syndicated radio show hosted by Barry Armstrong.

*If you have a truly superior product, then make sure it's priced that way!* Before IBD launched in 1984, Paine Webber analyst J. Kendrick Noble Jr. said O'Neil should recognize that "there isn't a mass audience for detailed stock information," *BusinessWeek* wrote in a Nov. 28, 1983, article. Noble thought he should try to sell a higher-price paper to a select market. Noble was right on the second point.

At the start, IBD charged $84 for a yearlong subscription. (Assuming 3% annual inflation, that's equivalent to $151 in 2004 dollars.) Problem was, it cost $84 whether you lived a few blocks from Wall Street, in Maine, or in the tiniest town in Nebraska or Alaska. There was no such thing as out-of-state subscription rates as the *New*

*York Times* had, which charged up to nearly $500 a year for those who lived outside New York.

In contrast, O'Neil sold 48 issues of "Long Term Values," which provided monthly charts on 4,000 stocks, for $195 a year. Surely, "Long Term Values" cost much less to produce than the paper. Yet "Long Term Values" subscriptions were more than twice as much! Daily Graphs also cost subscribers more than the paper.

"People don't realize what a bargain they are getting for all this stock information!" O'Neil said. "The biggest mistake we made was that we were under-priced."

The tables have turned in a way. IBD gives a discount for those who take on two- or three-year subscriptions. But rather than cut prices, it's raised the subscription price several times in the past few years to better reflect the quality of the information. Experienced readers know that one good trade can more than pay for the subscription. Meanwhile, the *New York Times* in April 2004 sent out direct-mail fliers offering an introductory rate of just $2.90 a week for the first three months.

For many years, IBD's all-day advanced seminar cost $795 to attend. IBD recently launched a brand-new seminar for the most advanced readers and investing professionals. The first one, held on April 17, 2004, included presentations by O'Neil and William O'Neil + Co. portfolio manager Steve Birch. They both discussed buying and selling rules and how to use charts. Readers got more chances to directly ask O'Neil questions than ever before. In addition, IBD's executive editor Chris Gessel taught new techniques on how to analyze the market's day-to-day action to grasp the overall direction, one of the keys to making money in the market. The seminar was limited to 200 seats. Each participant paid $2,995 for the whole-day seminar at the Century Plaza Hotel in Los Angeles. It sold out fast.

*If you discover a profit assumption to be incorrect, change course fast!*
In 1987, O'Neil guessed that IBD would break even when circulation

reached 125,000 to 130,000. In the second half of 1990, when the paper broke the 100,000 mark according to ABC figures, O'Neil raised the estimate to 200,000 readers. According to media reports, O'Neil in late 1992 said the paper, which had a circ of around 150,000, needed 250,000 to go into the black. The target later rose to 500,000. IBD's circ topped with the Nasdaq in early 2000.

This assumption has proven costly for years. O'Neil hired the Boston Consulting Group (BCG) in 2001 to look at the paper's circulation and fulfillment processes. But he didn't show the team a profit/loss statement, and he thought that the marketing department didn't need to make any changes, says David Sharpe, who led BCG's project team at IBD. "Bill's focus at that point when we came in was almost purely on growing circ," Sharpe said.

O'Neil's thinking was that if IBD could hit 500,000 in terms of circulation, then the advertisers couldn't ignore the paper anymore. The jump in ad revenue would push the paper into profitability. However, O'Neil and his executives failed to look at the crux of any business: Is it making a profit? If not, how can it?

During the 1990s and early 2000s, IBD's telemarketing wing, DMSI, aggressively gave discounts and other goodies to entice a few people who really didn't want to get a business paper. Many of these likely wouldn't have taken the time every day or week to study it and learn how to use it correctly. As a result, the cost of obtaining a subscriber shot well past the lifetime value of a customer. If the cost exceeds the value, you ain't profitable.

O'Neil was well aware of the rising costs. But since he had great cash flow from his other businesses, he figured it was all right and thought, "Let's go after the *Journal* in terms of circulation." But the bubble burst in 2000. IBD and the rest of the industry took hits in full-price subscriptions and ad revenue. In recent years, Sharpe and others noticed that O'Neil has shown a new way of thinking about the business as a whole.

"I think that, and I've never talked with him about this, Bill took a step back and said, 'What's the measure of success in business? Is it owning a sports team that loses money, or is it being profitable at doing what you're doing?' " said Sharpe, who in May 2004 joined IBD as senior vice president in charge of financial and strategic planning.

"And I think he started to measure himself along the profitability line, which caused this shift and this slow letting-go of a pure circulation goal. And today, we have more customers than we had a year ago."

Due to these strategic changes, IBD is no longer a one-size-fits-all product. It now has a product line that continues to grow. For people who don't want to shell out $295 for the paper but are still curious, they can get only the Monday edition or SmartLink for much less. If they like what they see and understand how IBD is different, they can attend a beginner-level seminar hosted by the paper. As they learn more, they can then invest money into additional higher-level products and services.

The point: IBD is a delivery device for outstanding stock and company information and an ongoing education on how to invest based on decades of research on the very best stocks of the past 50 years. Switching to the business model of delivering it cheaply and quickly rather than just doing nearly anything to boost the circulation numbers has helped boost IBD's profitability.

*When necessary, have the courage to turn your strategy 180 degrees around.* IBD was slow to go online. When Chris Gessel, IBD's markets editor, proposed a paperless paper in the late 1990s, O'Neil dismissed the idea at first. The idea slowly took hold, though, and over time became a project involving several managers. When IBD launched eIBD, a fully online version of the paper, in the summer of 2002, it was priced at $295. It was $60 higher than the hard-copy version at the time.

Why?

One IBD official said the team hoped to maximize profit from the online version in order to mop up as much as possible of the losses in the print version. It also didn't want to make the same mistake of being underpriced. Another manager pointed out that there were concerns over how advertisers would react to a fully electronic version of the paper.

When the Boston Consulting Group looked at the issue in 2003, it immediately advised O'Neil to make the price of eIBD lower than the paper. Why? Simple—eIBD cost less to distribute to readers, so it had a better profit margin than the paper product. For the company to achieve profitability, it made total sense to make eIBD cheaper and thus attract more customers.

This was hard to swallow for some. O'Neil loves to mark up the paper with a pen, circling a boldfaced stock in the tables here, drawing a trend line on the Nasdaq there, writing notes on a "New America" story and so on. Although technology is letting people scribble on PC screens, it's still a lot easier to doodle on paper for now. Some have worried that a smaller print circulation could impact ad revenue as more people migrate to the online version. Yet IBD has realized it can no longer defy the cold hard laws of business.

"If you're spending most of your marketing expenses on your most unprofitable product, then you'll find yourself in a rabbit hole that's hard to get out of," said Jessica Jensen. The BCG team of five consultants helped convince O'Neil that a carefully planned reduction in circulation of the paper version of IBD accompanied by growth in the electronic version is good, not bad.

As of May 2004, a one-year subscription to eIBD costs $235, which is $60 cheaper than the paper version.

*Market your product only to those who are actually interested in your product.* Have you ever gotten a CD-ROM from America Online, asking you to try 1,045 hours free? Did you get six of them over the past few years, or even a dozen? I got so many of them that I considered plastering one of my windows with the shiny discs. Eventually they ended up in a Los Angeles landfill.

Well, IBD didn't shell out as many freebies to consumers directly. But it did waste money sending CD-ROMs, videotapes and glossy direct mailers to many who probably weren't that interested in subscribing to a do-it-yourself investing paper.

IBD is expensive. It takes time—often years—to learn how to use it, master all the rules and make more money with the techniques. Most of the people who have done well with the paper have shelled out thousands of dollars to get IBD's sister product Daily Graphs Online® or to attend a couple IBD seminars. So why send an introductory video to someone who might not even spend 20 minutes studying stock prices? IBD bought lists of leads from vendors, but the lists were too broad. So retention became a problem.

"We were marketing to a lot of people who had few investible assets, who weren't investing in the market, and who weren't subscribing to a newspaper," Jensen said. "Rather than do a so-called carpet bombing, we have focused on targeted marketing."

Through its surveys and research, IBD now has a better grasp of who are its loyal readers and who is getting a lot out of the paper and related products. IBD's marketing team also quit the CD-ROM project after doing a study that showed that it did not make any impact on converting sales.

IBD also requires those who wish to take a four-week free trial of eIBD, IBD's online version, to submit a credit card account number during the registration. The potential customer does so with the understanding that after the free trial, the reader's account will be charged for a monthly online subscription unless he or she notifies IBD and wishes to cancel the trial. This feature, called a "four-week negative option," helps narrow the pool of potential future subscribers, says Ralph Perrini, IBD's vice president in charge of marketing.

*Avoid getting in big debt.* The opportunity to borrow money remains one of the underlying strengths of the U.S. economy. But taking out a big loan puts a strain on one of your biggest assets: time. Every new business needs time to succeed. It may take an extra year or two or three until your business moves from the red to the black. But if the bank doesn't give you that extra time, the chances of success fall sharply.

"We didn't owe any money to anyone," O'Neil said.

*Staying positive and upbeat all the time isn't a choice.* Terri Chiodo, IBD's national advertising director, says she benefited greatly by following the "10 Secrets To Success" O'Neil developed. (See Chapter 5 for more on this.) Number 5 is *Be persistent and work hard:* Success is a marathon, not a sprint. Never give up."

"I worked on it for a long time," Chiodo said. "Mr. O'Neil has always guided me in the principles of positive thinking."

During the drive to work, Chiodo listened to tapes of experts such as Dale Carnegie, Brian Tracy and Dr. Wayne Dyer. Chiodo says these principles paid off when she wooed Infiniti to advertise in IBD. She eventually got to meet Tom Orbe, who was general manager of Infiniti and sold him on the fact that IBD has a low duplication with the *Wall Street Journal* in terms of ad viewers. Later on, Infiniti's ad director came up with an innovative idea—tie in the car maker's brand with IBD's "10 Secrets To Success" by showing how its cars reflect and illustrate secrets such as "No. 6, Learn to analyze details," and "No. 8, Don't be afraid to innovate: Be different."

*Even if you have an outstanding product, innovate, innovate, innovate!* Intel co-founder Andy Grove perhaps said it best with his book, "Only the Paranoid Succeed." In the race of business, if you sit still, you could become the hare who loses to the tortoise. While IBD's Earnings Per Share and Relative Strength ratings were both revolutionary when they made their debut in the paper in April 1984, IBD has made a habit of continuing to look for ways to enhance its product.

The following are some of the major new innovations that IBD has made over the past 20 years:

**197 Industry Groups™ Table,** December 1984. This list of 197 different industry groups, which is owned by William O'Neil + Co., Inc., and is used by IBD under license agreement, is ranked daily in terms of six-month price performance. It has helped pioneer the analysis of industry group strength as a key factor of the most successful stocks. The Industry Group Relative Strength Rating was later added to the main stock tables.

**U.S. Treasury Bond Yield Curve Chart,** December 1985. IBD was the first publication to offer this to readers, say's O'Neil. It consisted of a line chart showing the yields of Treasury bonds having various time maturities as well as two more lines showing what yields were at 4 weeks and 13 weeks earlier. IBD also began printing charts of key commodities.

**New-highs List, Sorted by Industry Sector,** July 1991. The typical U.S. newspaper simply spits out in one list all the NYSE-listed stocks that hit 52-week highs. O'Neil discovered after years of study that up to 50% of a great stock's rise can be attributed to the strength of its industry group and the strength of its overall industry sector. When a new bull market kicks into gear, certain industries tend to come out of the gate faster. The best stocks in these industries make the biggest gains.

By separating all stocks, including those trading on the Nasdaq, that make new highs into their respective sectors, IBD has made it easier for investors to spot where the real growth of the market is taking place. No other publication shows the new-highs list this way. On July 29, 1991, the first day IBD published the list in this new format, the medical sector was among those featuring the most number of stocks hitting 52-week highs. Merck, Teva Pharmaceuticals and Surgical Care Affiliates made the list, and went on to superior gains in the 1990s.

**Accumulation/Distribution Rating,** March 1992. This letter rating (A is best, E is worst) tracks intraday moves in both price and volume to indicate whether a stock is being accumulated by institutional investors, the no. 1 driver of stock prices in the market. It covers 13 weeks of price-and-volume action. No other publication has anything that even remotely resembles this rating. Studies of the best growth stocks show that a stock tends to have an Accumulation/Distribution Rating of A or B before taking off on the biggest part of its price run. "It is more accurate than a simple up-down volume calculation," O'Neil said in an interview.

Most of the big market leaders of the 1990s showed an Accumulation/Distribution Rating of E in the spring and summer of 2000 before they rolled over and collapsed in the three-year bear market that followed.

**The New America,** April 1994. On this page, the stories on individual companies don't cover what's already big and mainstream. So you likely won't find articles on Microsoft and Intel, terrific stocks in previous decades but now too big to steadily outperform the market these days. Sure, these firms are key because they serve as the diplomats representing huge, rapidly changing industries.

New bull markets always feature new great stocks. These have little name recognition on Main Street, but they have the strongest year-over-year growth in earnings and sales. So they go on a first-name basis with the savviest mutual funds, hedge funds, banks and insurers. These new great stocks have a revolutionary new product or service that no one else has, and they're riding a tidal wave of profits and sales.

America is 228 years old, yet the fruits of a free-market economy keep giving the country fuel to constantly change and innovate. New companies rise and challenge the old guard. Even tragic events such as 9-11 spur the growth of new industries. "The New America" is totally about change and how to profit from that change.

**New Buys of Top Rated Funds,** April 1998. IBD took mutual funds rated A+ to A-, looked at its new buys and add-on buying of current positions, and then ranked the resulting holdings by combined EPS and RS ratings. This feature has helped readers identify the best-performing stocks. A separate feature looks at the latest sells of the top performing funds.

**SMR Rating (Sales Growth + Profit Margins + Return on Equity),** October 1998. Another letter rating (A is best, E is worst), this helps readers save time in finding companies with the best fundamentals. Those who say IBD is a pure-momentum shop are *completely wrong*. Roughly 60% of the components of a truly terrific stock are linked to the company's business prowess, not its stock action.

**IBD Stock Checkup,** July 2000. Found on www.investors.com, it gives a letter grade to every stock in IBD's database and diagnoses its fundamentals, technicals and the strength of the stock's industry group compared to the entire market.

**Stocks Highlighted in Yellow,** October 2001. IBD used a proprietary formula based on studies of the best stocks from 1953 to 2001 and highlighted stocks that showed similar characteristics by highlighting them in yellow in the Nasdaq and NYSE main tables. This feature was later changed to "Stocks in Black Bars." This feature helps investors sift quickly through the main tables to find stocks with the strongest fundamentals.

**IBD WebLink,** April 2002. In this exclusively online feature, markets writers examine the positive and negative elements of a stock's daily or weekly chart and write comments directly on the chart. They also analyze the stock's IBD "Checkup." The daily feature points out the pivot point, or the correct buy point, for a stock that's on the verge of making a new rally, and sell signals caused by a stock's price-and-volume action. It has served as a powerful tool to educate investors on how to use charts to beat the market and keep losses small. In 2003, WebLink identified fistfuls of big winners before they broke out of their bases and rocketed to new highs. They included Harman International, Nam Tai Electronics, Coach, OmniVision Technologies, Dick's Sporting Goods and Yahoo. All of these stocks gained 100% to 200% or more in 2003. This feature is now called the "Daily Stock Analysis."

**The IBD 100,** April 2003. This weekly feature ranks the 100 best companies in terms of growing fundamentals and stock-price strength. Readers can better understand the action of the market by studying which stocks make and stay on the list. It is *not* a buy list, but a batch of prospects worth carefully checking out and studying further. IBD also launched SmartLink in September 2003 and eTables in April 2004 to offer new readers a taste of IBD's research at a lower price point.

# CHAPTER 4

# Filling a Vacuum in a Crowded Media Universe

IBD has strong views on politics, foreign policy, taxes and the economy. It is, as the CNBC cable news show team of Larry Kudlow and Jim Cramer has pointed out, pro-growth, pro-company, pro-economy. These opinions aren't simply the personal views of a band of editors and writers. IBD has developed its own unique editorial voice through a decades-long search for facts. It has done an exhaustive analysis of the U.S. economy. IBD has also closely studied which government policies and programs truly enrich citizens' lives and which ones don't.

So it may come as a surprise that back in April 1984, IBD tried to launch itself as a paper free of opinion and official viewpoints.

*Investor's Daily* has no political biases. We don't advocate any political philosophy, and we have no political axes to grind in our news columns. We're here to provide impartial, accurate and relevant information about business, the economy and the markets to the millions of Americans who are concerned about their financial futures.

—From "Why A New Business Newspaper?"
front page of IBD, April 9, 1984

IBD tried hard to keep its pledge. For years, IBD didn't run regular editorials. The top story on the front page was a daily round-up of action on the NYSE. The "At the New York Analysts" front-page feature reported earnings announcements by various companies and the latest Wall Street earnings forecasts. A column called "Your Portfolio" revolved around topics on mutual funds, investing and real estate. IBD staff also wrote features on the stock market, emerging industry trends and the workplace.

The paper's promise didn't last long.

On July 31, 1984, just four months into the paper's launch, O'Neil penned an editorial criticizing what he viewed as narrow-minded thinking by economists on the economy.

What have you been told by Wall Street economic experts in the last year? The horrible, terrible deficit was going to result in much larger inflation and, as a consequence, soaring interest rates. The *Wall Street Journal* surveyed business executives and reported 90% of them felt the deficit was the No. 1 problem in America. Early in the cycle we were told the economic recovery wasn't so strong, and even such an expert as Milton Friedman . . . warned the recovery could soon fall into recession.

What really happened? Our economy is far stronger than predicted, and inflation has fizzled. What are the causes of such questionable future-telling? Economists try to predict what they think ought to happen in the future based on their theories. Instead, they should probably be concentrating their efforts on trying to recognize and completely understand what is actually happening at the time.

Overemphasis is placed on one key or pet indicator to explain or justify broad economic events. For example, Friedman, who is unquestionably one of our better economists, took the adamant stance that money supply is the only real cause of inflation. He ruled out the phenomenal oil price increases in the 1970s as an important contributing cause and called them a temporary aberration. With such thinking achieving wide acceptance, we can begin to understand why the country and the Federal Reserve Board developed paranoia over weekly money supply figures and our large deficit.

—From "How Can Such Bad Advice Come Out Of Wall Street?" July 31, 1984, IBD

O'Neil offered two different reasons why interest rates were still so high. One was that deregulation in the financial industry spurred many lenders to offer money market accounts with high interest yields to lure customers. So for a bank to stay in business, it has to charge higher interest rates on loans. The second reason was that the Federal Reserve may have kept the money supply too tight, fearing that "a strong economy would rekindle inflation." O'Neil called this nonsense.

Under this thinking, if the real gross national product is better than expected, that's bad; if worse than expected, that's good; because under their commonly held (and likely incorrect) thesis, a higher GNP means we must always have higher inflation. That's somewhat like telling your kids making A's and B's is bad because it must lead to no good and C's and D's are great because you're not overworked.

—From "How Can Such Bad Advice Come Out Of Wall Street?" July 31, 1984, IBD

So, what really happened?

The back of inflation was broken in March 1982 when oil prices began to fall. When Reagan removed natural-gas price controls, energy prices came down—to everyone's disbelief, O'Neil recalls. The market, which is smarter than any one individual or investor, understood this early. On Aug. 23 that year, the major indexes bolted higher and staged a key follow-through, confirming a new bull market was getting started. Ever since then, interest rates have been posting cyclical lows. The stock market and the economy roared for nearly two decades. And so far, inflation has never gotten as bad as it was in the early 1980s.

After a few years in the newspaper business, O'Neil realized that the paper had a certain responsibility to state relevant facts and argue against commonly held misconceptions about the economy and other issues. Perhaps that's one reason why O'Neil didn't mind the newspaper's losses year after year. He recognized its value as a key tool to spread truth about how things really work in the economy.

Some say that what made IBD's arguments in the editorials arena even more compelling is the fact that IBD came not from a publishing background but rather a stock market research background. O'Neil's success in the real world of business and investing gave the paper a sturdy foundation upon which to offer something unique and valuable to the national debate.

## Sick of the Media's Imbalance

O'Neil came from a family of Democrats. He voted for Jimmy Carter for president in 1976. But O'Neil, disappointed by what he calls "incompetent management" of the country, didn't vote for Carter again in 1980. Like almost the rest of the country, he chose Reagan. O'Neil also spotted an extreme bias in the mainstream media, one that favored the liberal view.

Take the Nicaragua conflict. There, the Marxist Sandinista guerillas waged war against the dictatorial government of Gen. Anastasio Somoza. By 1979, the nation was in civil war. Somoza fled the country. The Sandinistas seized Managua in July that year.

The threat of communism in America's backyard grew. The new Sandinista government aided leftist guerillas in El Salvador. The U.S. responded by backing anti-Sandinista guerilla groups called the *contras*. These guerillas could hardly be called warriors, though. Most were teenagers holding cheap rifles.

One day, a CBS News television correspondent reported the latest news on the conflict from Nicaragua. The man spoke while standing next to a tank in the battlefield—not one used by the contras but a Soviet tank manned by the Sandinistas. This bothered O'Neil.

"It was clear they [some of the U.S. media] were on the other side," O'Neil said in an interview. "These contras were mainly young people trying to get their country back. I remember President Reagan making speeches supporting the contras, but the media hardly covered them."

O'Neil also saw the media's leftist leanings when the U.S., with Reagan at the helm, invaded Grenada in October 1983 and confronted the Soviet Union and Cuba's expansion efforts on other fronts. Most Americans back then were unaware of the strong bias, O'Neil says. But now, O'Neil's observations have been well documented in a number of books.

In "The Media Elite," coauthors S. Robert Lichter, Stanley Rothman and Linda Lichter showed in a study of 240 key U.S. journalists that more than 80% of them voted for Democratic presidential candidates in the 1964, 1968, 1972 and 1976 elections. The 2003 book "Bias" by CBS news insider and Emmy Award winner Bernard Goldberg exposed how media executives gave a liberal slant to news and reporters simply regurgitated the views of liberal groups on controversial issues.

As the paper grew, O'Neil realized he could use IBD as a vehicle to provide a fresh viewpoint of the issues at hand. Today, he doesn't participate in the daily editorial meetings, but he does present ideas to editor Wes Mann occasionally. The editorial team in recent years has shown at times a libertarian streak, even though O'Neil himself is not a libertarian. "Government does have a place in society and it's important, but sometimes they're not very efficient," O'Neil said in an interview.

In any case, the strong views have perhaps hurt IBD's circulation growth. According to one IBD executive, there is "plenty of anecdotal evidence" showing that some investors like IBD's stock market data and investment philosophy but will not subscribe to the paper out of principle to protest the conservative editorial stance. The executive has suggested to O'Neil that he consider reducing the editorial content in order to help grow the product.

## No Longer Just an Investing Daily

Seven years into publication, it had become obvious that what then was known as the *Investor's Daily* had evolved into something more than simply a stock market newspaper. Circulation was growing fast, and many readers were depending on the paper not only for business news. They also hungered for coverage of important national issues, decision makers and management trends, says editor Wes Mann. After all, one of every five subscribers, in fact, didn't just work for companies or businesses; they *ran* them.

To reflect its more comprehensive content, *Investor's Daily* on Sept. 16, 1991, was renamed *Investor's Business Daily*. From that day on, in-depth coverage of a key national issue appeared daily at the top of the front page. The idea? Examine a major issue not just once a week, or even once a month as in other periodicals, but every day, 250 days a year.

"When the new format was first introduced, the "National Issue" story alternated with a "Corporate Performance" story in which a fast-growing company was examined," Mann said. "The first company to appear, on Sept. 17, 1991, was Amgen, the biotechnology leader that turned out to be the best stock of the last 20 years."

The first "National Issue" story dealt with the ramifications of a tax burden that had doubled in 50 years. Other early topics ranged from lagging productivity in U.S. manufacturing to America's low savings rate, from cost overruns in Medicare to the lack of accountability in the nation's schools, from rising poverty to the effectiveness of Fed policy.

The "National Issue" feature "came into being for much the same reason the newspaper did," said Mann, who became the paper's editor in 1988. "Just as investors needed more relevant and useful information on the financial market, Americans needed a more thorough and even-handed examination of the problems of the day."

Almost all the agenda setting in those days was done by media outlets in New York and Washington, and a certain mindset had taken hold. IBD refused to follow the crowd. Instead, it examined many of the same issues from a contrarian approach, raising points and asking questions that simply weren't being raised or asked. IBD also challenged conventional wisdom whenever and wherever the facts warranted.

The story on America's oft-lamented low savings rate, for example, looked at how other measures of savings and wealth—from stock to home ownership—had exploded. Another story looked with a jaundiced eye on the widely hyped industrial policies of Germany and Japan. And so it went on IBD's front page: major issues under the microscope, day in and day out, year in and year out.

"IBD's basic mission was always to help people. By the early 1990s, the mission had expanded into helping people manage: manage their investments, yes, but also manage their businesses and their lives," Mann said.

"But we were also trying to help the country manage—by providing more complete coverage on issues that were going half-analyzed, if they were analyzed at all. If it weren't for IBD, many issues—or sides of issues—would never have seen the light of day," Mann said.

The headlines atop the "National Issues"—often in the form of head-turning questions—illustrated IBD's contrarian approach: "Can Government Create Jobs?" "Can Trade Really Be Managed?" "Can Price Controls Lower Health-Care Costs?" "Will New Taxes Erase Red Ink?" "Is Planet Earth Really Doomed?"

## A Developed Voice

IBD's aggressive pursuit of national issues was carried over into editorials. The pieces started to appear on a regular basis with the paper's 10th anniversary in 1994. Circulation grew 20% that year in the teeth of one of the worst publishing cycles ever. IBD also added a section on "The Economy" and increased its coverage of "Companies In The News."

The first regular editorial, which ran on a weekly basis before later becoming a daily feature, appeared on April 12, 1993. Titled "Will Your Industry Be Next?" it noted how many industries—drugs, insurance, cable TV, liquor—had already been singled out by the brand-new Clinton White House for higher taxes, more regulation and/or other forms of harassment:

> The telecommunications industry also got a wake-up call. It came from Edward J. Markey, chairman of the House telecommunications subcommittee, who predicted that the FCC under Democrats would be "a tough cop on the beat."
>
> It will police the telephone companies," Markey promised. "It will police AT&T."

Only a few days earlier, Markey drew a bead on the mutual fund industry. He thinks it needs "federal attention" in view of its "astonishing growth during the last 10 years."

No telling what industry is next, but a pattern is emerging.

If it's an industry that's doing well—making money, creating jobs, keeping America competitive—chances are it'll find itself between *Congress' or Clinton's* crosshairs sooner rather than later.

Productive citizens of all economic strata have already gotten the message. Now business is getting it as well: Success in the Clinton era is something to be punished, not encouraged.

—From "Will Your Industry Be Next?"

April 12, 1993, IBD

The second editorial came a week later. Titled "Btu, VAT, Sin, Etc., Etc.," it deplored all the new tax plans the administration was cooking up. The third—"The President Who Cried Wolf"—objected to Clinton's raising every issue to "crisis" status. First, it was the economy, then the deficit, then health care, then jobs—all in the face of strong data showing facts in clear conflict with his ever-expanding agenda.

The fourth editorial regretted the president's abandonment of the middle class at the same time he was being hailed as a "New Democrat" with centrist leanings. "Rather than an administration of moderate and mainstream thinkers," IBD observed in the May 3, 1993, piece, "we get a Cabinet full of lawyers, lobbyists and leftists with ideas even more radical than those a majority of Americans have rejected repeatedly for the last 25 years."

By mid-May, the die was cast. An editorial titled "The Dog Ate My Credit Card" looked bemused on all the head scratching over why consumer confidence and spending had suddenly tailed off. To the editors at IBD, the reason was clear as crystal:

Americans face such a bewildering and frightening array of
new taxes that they can hardly be blamed for thinking
twice before buying anything, let alone new clothes, appli-
ances or homes. If others won't say it, we will: This is the
most anti-business, anti-growth, anti-entrepreneur, anti-
taxpayer and, yes, anti-consumer administration in modern
times.

## Fighting against Big Government

By the time Hillary Clinton's plan to reform the health-care system
surfaced later that spring, IBD had hit its stride, Mann says. Over the
next eight months, in no fewer than 38 front-page "National Issue"
stories, IBD examined and critiqued the plan from practically every
angle.

The White House insisted too many folks had no insurance and
that health-care prices were out of control. At the time, the mainstream media found little to question. But IBD looked at the data sur-
rounding the White House claims and laid it all out Oct. 25, 1993,
under the headline: "The Health-Care Crisis Myth: Medical Inflation,
Uninsured Below 1980s Rates." Even earlier, IBD asked the question, "Who Really Lacks Health Care?" and answered: "Most Of The
37 Million Uninsured Won't Be For Long."

All the while, the editorial page was weighing in with more than
two dozen analyses of its own. And by the time the plug was pulled on
the Clintons' attempt to take over one-seventh of the U.S. economy,
IBD was widely credited with an assist, Mann says. Here's an excerpt
from the one that ran on Aug. 2, 1993:

Anyone who's dealt with an unresponsive bureaucracy already
knows what our nation's health-care system will look like
under President Clinton's reform proposal.

Despite the lofty goal—guaranteed coverage for all—the delivery of health care under the Clinton plan will, in practice, look a lot like the delivery of any government service.

It's important to understand the Clinton plan is not merely a humanitarian effort to meet the health-care needs of the 37 million Americans who are believed to be uninsured.

Rather, it is a frontal assault on the American medical system, one that, if successful, will undermine existing—and efficient—private-sector arrangements between employer and employee. Under the president's plan, a government-run local "health alliance" will choose among competing "provider networks" to determine which will serve all of the residents of a particular community.

Consumers will not be permitted to choose a plan that isn't backed by the health alliance. Nor will they be allowed to buy "catastrophic insurance plans" with high deductibles and low premiums.

They will, as the head of the nation's physicians and surgeons told the administration's task force earlier this year, have the "sham choice of picking Monolith A or Monolith B, both offering the same government-dictated benefits package."

Because of its unknown cost and the Orwellian way it will intrude in all of our lives, health-care reform is already the subject of a hard sell by the administration.

—From "Health Reform's Hard Sell,"
Aug. 2, 1993, IBD editorial

Not every article in IBD criticized Clinton. The paper supported his stance on free trade and reforming welfare. O'Neil and crew were adamantly against the government program that gave funds to inner-city single mothers for each baby as long as no man resided in the household. The result? More homes and families broke up, O'Neil says.

"It really doesn't make that much of a difference which party is in the White House," O'Neil said. "The American economy usually does well. However, many well-intended government programs are not very effective and are very inefficient."

IBD also highlighted key changes in the Clinton White House's technology policy. In December 1996, IBD interviewed Sally Katzen, who was hired by Clinton to oversee billions of dollars worth of information technology projects taking place at federal agencies.

## Contrarian Wisdom

IBD's aggressive pursuit of issues in both the "National Issue" and editorial spots continued through the 1990s, a decade in which conventional wisdom—and the media that traded in it—really got a black eye.

Reviews that other newspapers did of their own forecasts heading into the 1990s were nothing less than sheepish.

"Most of the speculation about the '90s," the *Los Angeles Times* admitted in a Dec. 26, 1999, piece, "turned out in hindsight to be absurdly wrong, or at least absurdly shortsighted in terms of peering into the future."

"The *Times*," it confessed, "along with everyone else pretty much missed the boat."

IBD, however, could hardly be included with "everyone else." In fact, its readers would be hard-pressed to remember anything from that 10-year period that was all that surprising. In case after case, IBD analyses of facts at hand—not conventional wisdom—often pointed to the eventual outcome.

Here is a sampling of "predictions" torn (as they say) from the pages of IBD over that decade:

## Low Inflation, Low Interest Rates

On Aug. 14, 1991, with the yield on the benchmark 30-year Treasury bond at 8.17%, the headline at the top of our front page read: "Is A New Era Of Low Interest Rates At Hand?"

A chart accompanying the story showed the Fed discount rate at a historic junction. One more reduction, it illustrated, would undercut the rate's cyclical low. Could the Fed and economic policymakers end a 45-year trend in which the rate had marched steadily higher, with each cyclical high and low higher than the last?

Yes! The trend reversed in the 1980s, when an increase in the middle of the decade fell far short of the stratospheric prior highs before turning down again. The bond never returned to its level at the beginning of the decade, and in the spring of 2004 stood 55% *lower*. The article pointed out the factors that could upset this new virtuous cycle: a policy that was antigrowth.

## The Decline of George Herbert Walker Bush

On Oct. 15, 1991, when the first President Bush still enjoyed the approval of two-thirds of the public, IBD asked at the top of the front page: "Can President Bush Be Beaten?" One could appreciate this bold question when considering that at the time, more Democrats were bowing out of a run for the White House than throwing hats in.

It wasn't entirely the recent slippage in the president's approval ratings (from their extraordinary Persian Gulf War highs) that prompted the question. It was the economy's persistent weakness under Bush's feckless leadership.

Bush Sr. raised taxes in a budget deal with Democrats. Although he had promised not to do that—"Read my lips: no new taxes"—he didn't put money where his mouth is. Bush raised reserve requirements for banks, which in turn caused a credit crunch. He also re-regulated certain parts of the economy via the Americans with

111

Disabilities Act. To some extent, the elder Bush re-regulated the country.

If IBD had had a regular editorial back then, its editorial writers likely would have slammed Bush for these moves.

Among the many ominous signs charted with the story: growth in personal income, which had plunged from 5% just before Bush was elected in 1988 to 1% (en route to negative territory in early 1992).

## The Salesmanship of Bill Clinton

A lot of readers didn't like IBD's pointing it out, any more than IBD liked pointing it out. But it became obvious early in the Clinton administration that the new president played fast and loose with the whole truth.

IBD's suspicion had nothing to do with private dalliances. (Monica Lewinsky, the White House intern with whom Clinton had a sexual affair, which he later denied repeatedly, was still in high school.) It had to do with Clinton's throwing around bogus "facts" about the economy to persuade a trusting public (and what turned out to be an inattentive press corps, says Mann) of whatever he was pushing at the time.

The examples piled up so high that IBD had to start a special column, "The President's Words," to separate rhetoric from reality. Declaring the economy he inherited the worst since the Great Depression was only the beginning, Mann says. At the time the president said this, the economy was actually revving back up to the point where, in a few short months, the Fed would be trying to cool it off with an unprecedented barrage of interest rate hikes.

"He would make six claims in one long convincing statement. Three or four would be true, and two or three would either be giant exaggerations or just not true. But since most were true, everything was accepted," O'Neil said. "He was a bright man and a great salesman."

IBD eventually dropped the column because it was unable to keep up with the volume of falsehoods and exaggerations coming out of the White House. Nevertheless, the paper continued to investigate and expose details on what it saw as a wide range of matters in which the Clintons bent the truth.

## The New America

Sometime in the late 1990s it dawned on the mainstream media that there were a lot of new companies out there. The newspaper giants began to realize that the new companies were having a major impact on how we go about our lives, on the job and off.

By then, attention had focused on the Internet. But the fact is, the U.S. had entered a new era of growth via tax incentives at least 15 years earlier, when it had started to reassert its global leadership not only politically and militarily but economically as well.

"The New America," as IBD was calling it even back then, was "one in which the entrepreneurial spirit that made the nation great is manifesting itself in thousands of newer companies with revolutionary new ideas, innovative new products, mind-boggling new technologies and vastly improved ways of doing business," O'Neil wrote in his fore-word to "The Investor's Business Daily Almanac 1992: The Facts, The Figures, The Trends."

These rapidly growing companies were "keeping the U.S. competitive and creating wealth for employees and shareholders alike. One by one, industry by industry, they have risen to challenge and overtake what were regarded as the old leaders."

These business dynamos continued to come public so fast that finally, in April 1994, IBD created an entire "New America" page to keep up with them. Studies show that companies showcased here tend to outperform the market. From Oct. 2, 1998, to June 22, 2004, the IBD New America Index of companies featured in the past six months was up 138%. Over the same time frame, the S&P 500 was up just 13%.

## The New Economy

As a natural outgrowth of the New America companies and dynamic industries came what IBD was among the first to call a "New Economy." What did that mean? Consider it a time of low inflation, high productivity and . . . innovation, innovation, innovation.

Mainstream pundits and economists were obsessed in the early 1990s with inflation. In 1996, they were warning that inflation would be a byproduct of what was then a surge in job growth, Mann says.

For years, economists believed in a fixed level of growth at which inflation picked up. Anything faster than 2.5%, they thought, was a violation of the economy's natural speed limit. This natural speed limit was called the *nonaccelerating inflation rate of unemployment*, or NAIRU.

IBD never believed it. In article after article, IBD showed its readers why NAIRU was faulty—and why the economy could grow much faster than the Fed or anyone else thought.

In stories like "Jobs Vs. Inflation" (Aug. 4, 1995), "Is Economy Near Speed Limit, Or Can GDP Rev Even Faster?" (March 25, 1996) and "Fear Of Jobs" (March 14, 1996), IBD argued that, thanks to the New Economy's gravity-defying investment surge, the U.S. could turn out more jobs, more growth and higher incomes—*without* an uptick in inflation.

Facts eventually bore this out. The GDP grew 4.5% in 1997, 4.2% in 1998, and 4.4% in 1999. Meanwhile, joblessness stayed well below 5%. Even after three years of exceeding the economy's so-called speed limit, inflation was a no-show.

## The Boom in Productivity

IBD also noted that surging profits at American companies suggested the U.S. was experiencing a "hidden productivity boom" (Sept. 22, 1997). Two years later, the government went back and redid all its data to find that the rate of productivity in the mid- to late 1990s was in fact much faster than thought. The productivity boom came out of hiding.

Other economic calls were just as prescient.

While others predicted the sky would fall when the Asian crisis gripped the world, IBD correctly pointed out (Oct. 6, 1997) that Asia's woes would boost the U.S. economy. Consumers would pay lower prices for foreign goods, IBD predicted, helping to keep inflation low and giving the economy room to grow. The following two years turned out to be a powerful period for growth—fueled by rapid consumer spending, low inflation and high investment.

As far back as 1995, people had been worried about a new Congress under Republican control for the first time in 40 years. What would happen if it balanced the budget? Wouldn't that kill the economy? Well, in February 1995—right after the new Congress was seated—IBD pointed out that a shrinking deficit would not kill growth—and that it was the size of the government, not the deficit, that mattered. In the years that followed, government as a share of the economy shrank, a surplus appeared and the economy thrived.

## The Ongoing Economic Boom and Bull Market

IBD's "National Issues" stories and editorials usually left it to others to predict the end of the record economic expansion and bull market of the 1990s. There was no shortage of gurus willing to do so. But in those rare instances in which the paper did feel the need to venture out, it was helpful.

115

As in July 1998, when fears of the "Asian contagion" were spreading rapidly, the CEOs we regularly surveyed assured us that the expansion would last at least through the end of 2000. Indeed it did.

Or on Sept. 1, 1998, when IBD declared, at the top of the front page, that the longest bull market in history had ended and that the first bear market in eight years (a bear most news organizations still hadn't acknowledged) was underway.

Or on Oct. 16, 1998, when IBD suggested as strongly as is journalistically prudent that the bear had suddenly ended, and that a new bull had begun.

Or, to cite a more recent example, on Oct. 11, 2002, the day after stocks finally bottomed out after the worst bear market in 70 years, when IBD raised the possibility of a rerun of 1990–91. Back then, the market bottomed in early October 1990 and then took off in January 1991, when bombs started dropping in Baghdad.

IBD's opinions haven't necessarily always been right or the most sound. The editorial policy recently became more flexible as well. On July 19, 2004, the Issues & Insights page began publishing a column from a liberal thinker not affiliated with IBD every Monday. That same day, it also started printing an editorial cartoon. The paper now embraces a wider range of opinions on political, social and economic issues.

But when it comes to spotting major shifts in the stock market, IBD's unique, fact-based analysis of stock action helps keep it ahead of the media herd. So does IBD's refusal to simply follow the crowd or the opinions of talking heads. This policy and the paper's understanding of how the economy really works may help keep IBD's editorial features on the cutting edge as well.

# CHAPTER 5

# Not All News Should Be Bad News

I am a mentor to a young boy, 13, who has no dad. I have met with him weekly for three years. I use the "Leaders & Success" column to develop messages for him that he can apply to his benefit. That this is working is no surprise I am sure, for as we think, so we are, but now that several of his friends have joined us in these discussions, it has been doubly gratifying. Thanks for your positive contribution to these kids' lives."

—Michael Burton, IBD subscriber

I also share most of them [articles in the L&S page] with my college-age kids to let them know that most successful people started out as average people, just like them.

—Jim Elder, IBD subscriber

I am truly impressed by "Leaders & Success." It is inspiring! My only disappointment is that your paper is only published five days a week, for Sunday and Monday I suffer with withdrawal.

I find the stories of successful people and demonstrations of personal courage and persistence very helpful and a light to my path. Never allow yourselves to even consider stopping the series."

—Tim Cotie, M.D., IBD subscriber

Bill O'Neil talks and acts like a gentleman. He picks words carefully. He doesn't curse in public.

But when he reminisced inside his office in April 2004 about how the "Leaders & Success" feature was born, O'Neil showed he's also an ordinary guy with emotions like anyone else.

"Five or six years ago, I did a study of front-page articles in the *LA Times* and other big-city papers," O'Neil recalled. He paused. "Dammit, seven out of eight stories were negative. They were about who got killed. Who got shot. Who got robbed. Who was arrested for drunk driving. What sexual deviant is out there.

"Then I opened the second page of the papers, then the third page, and the fourth page. You know what was in there? The same old negative stuff! Holy cow!"

O'Neil, and perhaps many newspaper readers, strongly felt that the press focused too much on the negative. By doing so, the media didn't properly reflect reality in society. He had enough.

O'Neil's idea of taking a more balanced approach to news isn't original.

Michael Bloomberg of *Bloomberg News* made a point of never including news of local murders, robberies and so forth on the Bloomberg computer terminals. Results of the latest Yankees game? Sure thing. A murder in New York City? Nope.

In October 1983, *USA Today* founder Al Neuharth proposed to the Overseas Press Club in New York that America begin a "new journalism of hope" to replace what he called "the old journalism of despair," Peter S. Prichard wrote in "The Making of McPaper: The

Inside Story of *USA Today*." Neuharth's thinking influenced some *USA Today* editors to emphasize the positive aspect of a news item as equally as the negative side. Ann Landers' syndicated column and its successor have helped people figure out how to deal with problems in a positive way.

But in the history of U.S. journalism, the "Leaders & Success" column is perhaps unique. Every day, the feature strives to inspire readers to set lofty goals, believe in their own dreams, and achieve their own greatness.

"I think it is a great feature, and fits in with the role IBD plays as a newspaper for investors and people who want to succeed in business. Choices [for the articles] are good and varied," said John Curley, in an interview via e-mail. Curley was executive editor of *USA Today* and later became CEO of the paper's parent, Gannett Co. He is currently a journalism professor at Pennsylvania State University.

"It belongs in the newspaper, given its mission. Every newspaper has beats that are designed for the readers it wants to serve, and that feature certainly appeals to readers who want to succeed."

Why did the L&S feature seem necessary in a business and financial newspaper?

"I didn't have many examples put in front of me when I was young. I just read and found these stories helped me tremendously," O'Neil said. He read everything he could find, and he was able to figure out a success strategy built around all of these role models. O'Neil recognized that discipline, motivation and positive thinking are not always intuitive. "If positive strategies were intuitive, everyone in the world would be an overachiever," he said.

O'Neil has always said the first reaction when there's a problem often is to blame someone else. It's easier for a person to do than focusing on his or her part in the matter. "It's human nature not to want to own up to some things, but it doesn't solve problems."

In February 1988, the L&S article ran in feature slot no. 2 on the front page. It tried to attract readers who were CEOs and top managers. The topics covered executive salaries, what to wear to work, pension benefits and child-care aid. After about a year, L&S disappeared. Then it came back to tackle the same kinds of issues before falling off the pages once more.

On Sept. 16, 1991, IBD changed its name to its present-day one from the original *Investor's Daily*. Just below the masthead were the words, *"The Newspaper For Important Decision Makers."* L&S went through yet another reincarnation. Only this time, each and every day on the front page it would profile "an important decision maker." The first article profiled Democrat Sen. Tom Harkin. Next came Patrizio Vinciarelli, who became a millionaire by inventing a zero-current switch after seeing his stereo go up in smoke in 1974; John Sawhill, president of the Nature Conservancy; and Assunta Ng, who founded the bilingual *Seattle Chinese Post*. She was honored by the Small Business Administration as "one of five women who overcame adversity to build successful businesses."

The stories described what these people do; what they're thinking now; what others think of them; where they come from; what they were like in school; and what their success means for the future of America. There were also a few tips on how they succeeded. In other words, there wasn't much of a focus. This went on for years. Then the L&S profile became more consistent in writing style, tone, content and purpose when it was wed with O'Neil's "10 Secrets to Success" on Sept. 15, 1998, and got its own page. These are the secrets:

1. *How you think is everything:* Always be positive. Think success, not failure. Beware of a negative environment.

2. *Decide upon your true dreams and goals:* Write down your specific goals, and develop a plan to reach them.

3. *Take action:* Goals are nothing without action. Don't be afraid to get started. Just do it.

4. *Never stop learning:* Go back to school or read books. Get training and acquire skills.

5. Be *persistent and work hard:* Success is a marathon, not a sprint. Never give up.

6. *Learn to analyze details:* Get all the facts, all the input. Learn from your mistakes.

7. *Focus your time and money:* Don't let other people or things distract you.

8. *Don't be afraid to innovate; be different:* Following the herd is a sure way to mediocrity.

9. *Deal and communicate with people effectively:* No person is an island. Learn to understand and motivate others.

10. *Be honest and dependable; take responsibility:* Otherwise, 1 to 9 won't matter.

O'Neil loved to read about the lives of famous and successful people in government, science, sports and business—folks like Winston Churchill, Thomas Edison, the Wright Bros., Abraham Lincoln, Teddy Roosevelt, Walt Disney, John D. Rockefeller, Alexander Graham Bell, Andrew Carnegie, J. C. Penney, Conrad Hilton and Bruce Jenner, the 1984 Olympic decathlon gold medalist. After years of study, he came up with these 10 traits. He actually had more, but he decided to stick to a round number. But O'Neil is mulling the idea of adding one or two more secrets because what astounds him is how even today, in the age of information, few people actually take these secrets to success to heart.

"Most people assume they have 8 of the 10 secrets to success," O'Neil said. "I think most are deficient in 8 out of 10. Someone will say, 'Oh yeah, I'm positive.' But if that person fails two or three times at something, he or she usually doesn't try again. Based on the people I studied, I found that the highly successful have all of the secrets."

"Could you imagine if young people were taught this in school?" O'Neil added, his eyes lighting up, his voice growing stronger. "It would be very, very good for them later in life."

O'Neil takes these lessons so seriously that in the 1990s to early 2000s, he had 50 or so plaques hung in the main hallway of the LA office, each inscribed with a pump-me-up saying on a brass plate like the following: "It's not the size of the dog in the fight that counts, it's the size of the fight in the dog." One staffer came up with the phrase: "Why not?" Some employees snickered at the pellets of wisdom, but others found inspiration. An illness once left Kathy Sherman bedridden, and the doctor told her she would never walk again. "I thought to myself, what would Bill O'Neil do? I told myself to stay positive," Sherman said. She proved the doctors wrong.

> Bill is an entrepreneur who thrives on innovation. The "Leaders & Success" page in IBD and its "10 Secrets to Success" are an open book to Bill and his thinking. Through the senior editors, we often hear he's said, "Come up with something new and better—don't copy." That's been very much on Bill's mind from the beginning.
>
> —Doug Rogers, mutual funds editor, IBD

The first feature on the new and improved "Leaders & Success" page on Sept. 15, 1998, presented Bill Gates, one of the world's most successful entrepreneurs in history, in a two-part series. The story focused on how Gates organizes his time:

It led to the biggest change in how Bill Gates runs Microsoft Corp. since he founded the company 23 years ago.

As Microsoft's 1998 fiscal year was drawing to a close in June, Gates sat down with his right-hand man, Steve Ballmer, and reviewed everything Gates had done in the prior 12 months.

Everything. From brainstorming products to budget reviews to golf club endorsements.

The yearly review mirrored the way Gates measures his efficiency every day.

Throughout the year, at the end of each day, Gates looks at what he could have cut out of his schedule.

Then, just in case he's missed something, just in case he's not being objective enough about his own performance, he takes the process one step further.

He has Ballmer look over what he's done and suggest how he could have used his time more effectively.

"Having someone do that and giving you very frank feedback is a great way to stay focused on what you aim to accomplish," Gates told IBD.

—Lisa Wirthman, "Microsoft's Bill Gates,"
first of two parts, Sept. 15, 1998, IBD

Now, many people have read about how successful people work hard, listen to others, keep their promises, and never give up. It's very easy for a cynic to look down on a feature such as L&S.

That's why Kinou Treiser, the first editor of the L&S page, and her successor, Joanne von Alroth, constantly pressed IBD writers to dig deep and find real stories of behavior and decisions that led to success. It's a lesson straight from Journalism Class 101: Show, don't tell. Such examples stick longer in readers' minds and may in fact help them change their ways for the better.

123

# IBD's 10 Secrets to Success, No. 10: Be Honest and Dependable; Take Responsibility

Yes, we've all heard that honesty is the best policy. But the opening paragraphs of Brian Mitchell's L&S profile on Dairy Queen's Harris Cooper, which won a story award during an in-house monthly contest run by senior editors in 1999, show this crucial trait of leadership in action:

> Harris Cooper had just finished a speech telling his franchisees in St. Louis everything that International Dairy Queen was going to do for them.
>
> A man from the audience came up afterward to talk with him.
>
> "I like what you're saying," he said, "but I've heard it so many times in this group that I can only say: The proof of the pudding will be in the eating."
>
> His words struck Cooper as a warning. He'd taken over as president and chief executive of IDQ just the previous year, 1970. The company was near bankruptcy, and Cooper had been hired to turn it around.
>
> He realized he couldn't do it if he couldn't keep his franchisees on board. He couldn't keep them on board if they didn't trust him to keep his promises.
>
> Cooper figured out a way to keep them on board, and he turned IDQ around. In his 17 years at the helm, IDQ's annual ad budget rose from $500,000 to $34 million. Outlets grew from 4,000 to 5,200 in the U.S. and from 300 to 450 in Canada. Last year Warren E. Buffett's Berkshire Hathaway, Inc., bought IDQ for $585 million.
>
> How did Cooper do it?
>
> First, he decided he needed to treat his mom-and-pop franchisees like customers. Too many franchisers and franchisees mistakenly think of each other as partners, Cooper,

61, says. "That's only true up until the day the franchiser sells his first product to the franchisee," he said.

That day the franchisee becomes a customer, "the only customer you have," Cooper said.

Treating the store owners like customers meant constantly working to sell them on the Dairy Queen brand and IDQ's supplies. It meant getting to know them and listening to their ideas.

"You've got to be where the people are making you the money," Cooper said. "You can't sit in an ivory tower and expect to tell mom and pop what to do."

Cooper estimates that he met with franchisees and suppliers about 250 times a year.

\* \* \*

Listening to franchisees paid off for Cooper. Many of the best ideas for products and marketing came from the front lines.

After listening to store owners' suggestions, IDQ added ice-cream cakes and logs and revived the chain's popular Peanut Buster Parfait. One franchisee, Sam Temperato of St. Louis, came up with the Full Meal Deal combination, More Burger Than Bun two- and three-patty hamburgers, and the Blizzard multiflavored milkshake.

A store-owner advisory board almost rejected the Blizzard. But Cooper intervened, suggesting a visit to Temperato's St. Louis stores to see how the Blizzard was selling. When board members saw the lines at the stores, they were sold.

—Brian Mitchell, "Dairy Queen's
Harris Cooper: Focus On Honesty Put
The Topping On His Career," Aug. 4, 1999, IBD

Cooper proved he was honest in his goals. Later in the story, Mitchell also showed how a mentor helped Cooper stay an honest manager:

The new IDQ board chairman was Bill McKinstry, who also had been a General Motors Corp. and Chrysler Corp. franchisee.

Cooper calls McKinstry his mentor on franchising. McKinstry said, for example, that Cooper should always start a visit with a franchisee by suggesting how that franchisee could make another dollar every day.

Cooper recalled McKinstry's saying, "You talk to that first. Anything else you want to talk to him about comes second, even if he owes you money."

McKinstry's second lesson: "Every default letter you write [terminating a franchise] is an indication of your lack of ability."

Cooper also learned from McKinstry to keep business relationships businesslike. McKinstry didn't expect employees to socialize together or encourage them to believe they belonged to a corporate family.

McKinstry, who has several daughters, once told Cooper, "You're like the son I always wanted, but if the numbers aren't there, you won't be here."

Cooper took the same approach in dealing with his moms and pops. "The business they're in is profits. It isn't Dairy Queen. That's just a conduit to what? Profits," he said.

"So you have to be honest with them," Cooper said. Anything you promise must be done. Don't be afraid to say, 'I don't know,' and get the answer later. In other words, don't lie and don't guess. Who can [beat you] if you play by those rules?"

Cooper was so respected by his franchisees that after he retired from IDQ, they hired him in 1991 to run their association and cooperative.

Not all L&S features are about businesspeople. Inventors, writers, poets, scientists, musicians, artists, past U.S. presidents, Nobel Peace Prize winners, doctors, military generals, teachers, civil rights activists and unusually gifted students all get their turn on the L&S page.

Many IBD writers have profiled top athletes and coaches as well, and no wonder. The stories of their dedication continue to inspire and astonish. Take Chris Warden's July 28, 1999, piece on Nolan Ryan, which won a "Top L&S Story" award that month:

> Most second-graders are asleep at 1 a.m. Not Nolan Ryan. He was busy helping his father, Nolan Sr., deliver the *Houston Post* on a route 55 miles long.
>
> The family needed his help, so Nolan would work with his dad till 4:30 a.m., catch a few more hours of sleep and then go to school after seeing his dad off to his day job as an oil field supervisor.
>
> It was that hard work that marked Ryan's 27-year career in Major League Baseball. He pitched more no-hitters, recorded more strikeouts and played more seasons than any other player. He holds or shares 50 other major-league records. He was voted into the Baseball Hall of Fame on the first ballot with the second-highest percentage of votes in history.
>
> —"Pitcher Nolan Ryan: Hard Work And Focus Helped Him Reach The Top," July 28, 1999, IBD

Like every other major-league pitcher, Ryan stood on the mound alone. Yet Warden pointed out how Ryan aimed to get the best advice from experts in his line of work.

When he joined the Houston Astros after the 1979 season—becoming the first million-dollar player—he knew that to get ahead, he'd need someone else to help him maintain his strength. He willingly put himself in the care of conditioning coach Gene Coleman.

"I think the impact that Tom Morgan had on my delivery and Gene Coleman and Tom House [of the Texas Rangers club, which Ryan joined in 1989] had on my conditioning was pivotal to my longevity," Ryan said in the *Los Angeles Times*.

"The challenge was in continuing to compete at that level against guys who were a lot younger than I was, and because of that I was willing to work and put in the additional hours," he said.

Once in a while, the L&S page comes up with a profilee that 99 out of 100 people have never heard of. Yet that person has touched millions of people's lives in some way. Gloria Lau's piece on Matthew Fontaine Maury, a September 1999 top story award winner, explains in fine detail how Maury mapped the entire ocean.

Though sailors in the early 1800s knew adverse winds or changes in currents could force a ship far off route, they had to endure. They knew favorable currents could double the ship's speed. But they had scant information. So trips were long, unwieldy and dangerous.

Oceanographer Matthew Fontaine Maury (1806–73) learned this as a U.S. Navy midshipman. During his nine-year tour of duty, he grew impatient with the lack of information on the sea. When he returned home to Fredericksburg, Va., he set out to turn seafaring into a science.

Maury wasn't the first to recognize the need for reliable navigating information, but he persisted where others had given up.

Centuries earlier, Greek sailors learned how to use the Aegean Sea's northerly summer winds and monsoons to make round-trip voyages to India easier.

Sailors in the 15th century learned to use both Atlantic and Pacific trade winds. In 1688, English astronomer Edmund Halley charted the ocean winds in the tropical regions. And Benjamin Franklin produced a map of the Gulf Stream in 1770. Others added knowledge, but none with Maury's thorough accuracy.

Seeing how much a complete map of the sea would aid captains fired his determination. Maury set out to map the entire ocean. When he took a job in 1842 to head the Depot of Charts and Instruments—today called the National Weather Service—Maury discovered thousands of logbooks compiled by captains after long voyages.

## Mined Logbooks

Although his predecessors hadn't thought to review the logbooks, he did. He mined them for data. The logs recorded wind, weather and currents on the captains' voyages. Others had been daunted by the piles of unordered books.

Maury persevered despite the intimidating task. He and his assistants examined more than 10,000 logs—a task that took more than five years.

"If he found that a ship encountered northwest winds in latitude 40 degrees north, longitude 60 degrees west in the month of July, Maury went through the log of every ship that had sailed near that spot in that month in the 60-odd years of his records to see what winds she encountered," wrote naval authority Harold Calahan.

Maury reasoned that if ships had found the same conditions for 60 years, future ships would likely find the same conditions at the same time in the same places.

> —"Oceanographer Matthew Fontaine Maury:
> His Perseverance And Determination
> Saved Merchants Time, Money And Lives,"
> L&S page, Sept. 2, 1999, IBD

Maury faced tons of skeptics, but he managed to change their beliefs by sharing his research with as many fellow sailors as possible.

He wanted to teach other sailors his methods to ease their voyages. In 1847, he published the Wind and Current Chart of the North Atlantic and handed out some 5,000 copies to skippers along the Atlantic seaboard.

It was one of three books and dozens of scientific articles he would write. To instruct sea captains further, he led international meteorological conferences.

Whenever possible, he added solid data to the records. After all, he reasoned, voyages would only be made easier if information improved. So he devised and printed thousands of blank charts in 1848.

He urged sea captains to use these blank charts to mark and track their ships from day to day, especially when they sailed over parts of the sea about which information was scarce.

Many times Maury had to fight skeptical sea captains. Traditionalists preferred to sail by instinct, the way it had always been done. But by persisting, Maury managed to convince more than 1,000 skippers.

For their help, he compensated sea captains by distributing 200,000 copies of the charts and 20,000 copies of sailing directions in book form.

Maury believed in himself and his maps. To convince skeptics, he calculated that the average sailing voyage from New York to Rio was typically 55 days. Using his directions, that trip shrank to just 40 days.

Eventually the skeptics believed. Maury prevailed with indisputable facts. Trips from New York to Lisbon were cut in half. A week was saved per trip to Dublin. And trips to San Francisco were sliced to 133 days from 180 days.

American shippers calculated that the charts collectively saved them more than $2 million a year. British shippers claimed they saved $10 million.


The L&S feature doesn't rank highly in reader surveys. In an April 2004 IBD survey, it ranked as the 53rd most frequently read story or feature in the paper. O'Neil argues that for a business paper, that *is* a high readership rate. In any case, IBD probably wouldn't be around today if it weren't for O'Neil's positive thinking in the first place.

"If you consider that 95% of our subscribers are doing so for the investment data, then it's unusually strong to have almost half, or 46.3%, say they read it regularly," O'Neil said.

In the spring of 2004, he told the paper's editors he wanted the paper to go back to two features a day. They weren't thrilled, to say the least.

In the end, they compromised. Since May 2004, the L&S page has gone back to two L&S features on days when there is no ad. But to keep a lid on freelance writing expenses, the second story runs under the subhead, "Best of Leaders & Success."

# IBD Founder William J. O'Neil

Keep Learning: Relentlessly positive, he says errors aren't just for baseball players.
—by Joanne von Alroth,
"Leaders & Success," April 19, 2004

The most valuable investment Bill O'Neil ever made was in a mistake.*

While stationed at Ladd Air Force Base in Fairbanks, Alaska, in the late 1950s, then-1st Lt. O'Neil and his wife, Fay, put their meager savings into the most common investment: property. The couple purchased a triplex, which they intended to sell for a profit when O'Neil finished his tour of duty and left Fairbanks.

But the building didn't sell quickly, and a local real estate agent persuaded O'Neil to let her handle the sale while he moved. A few swift, shady deals followed, and the real estate agent swindled the young pair out of their hard-earned investment.

O'Neil was incensed. Rather than stay angry, though, he decided to look at the loss as a watershed moment. "I said, 'I'm going to make a lot of money out of this because I've learned my lesson,'" he recalled. "I didn't check that real estate agent out enough. I didn't do my research. I didn't have all the facts. But I decided I'd never make that mistake again."

O'Neil believes, in fact, that making a mistake—a really big one—is one of the best ways to learn.

"With one little mistake, it doesn't dawn on you what you did wrong," he said. "You have to really blow the whole thing, then figure out exactly where you went wrong. Then you change things. And you adjust until you get it right."

---

*The quotes in this section are from von Alroth interviews for "Leaders & Success," April 19, 2004.

## The Right Attitude

It's a formula that's served him well: O'Neil, the founder of *Investor's Business Daily*, has become one of the world's greatest investors. Today he's the chairman of Data Analysis Inc., the holding company for IBD and sister firms William O'Neil + Co., a leading institutional investment research and brokerage firm; O'Neil Data Systems, a diversified commercial printing company; and Daily Graphs Inc., a widely used online and print stock charting service.

How'd he do it? Ask O'Neil, and he'll tell you that much of it is the result of one word: attitude.

"I never met anyone, or heard of anyone, or read of anyone who was successful who was a pessimist," said the energetic 71-year-old. "You have to be positive, or you'll never get anywhere."

His attitude is near legendary among those he works with. "He's very, very positive," said William O'Neil + Co.'s chief financial officer Don Drake, who's worked with O'Neil since 1975. "He knows that if the leader is positive, so is everyone else."

Without O'Neil's push-forward viewpoint, his business wouldn't exist, Drake said. "When I joined the company, it had been losing money, and a lot of others thought he'd go out of business," Drake said. "He could've walked away, but he didn't. Instead, he said, 'We'll find a way through this,' and he changed what needed to be changed until it worked."

"He will always turn a negative into a positive, no matter how much the world is falling down around him," agreed Connie Cullen, William O'Neil + Co.'s executive vice president, director of data research. "And if you start talking negatively, he gets upset, and he'll tell you you're undermining yourself."

O'Neil's approach isn't naturally ingrained. He's no happy-go-lucky Pollyanna.

"I don't think there's very many natural-born anythings," he said. "You have to train yourself to be what you want to be."

That's how he became an optimist. As a young salesman, O'Neil suffered from shyness. The best way to overcome it, he figured, was to learn from those who were already good at public speaking—members of the Toastmasters Club.

He watched and listened carefully at meetings. He went home and practiced his speaking, returning to meetings to get critiques. He maintained the routine until he was comfortable speaking to one and all.

O'Neil didn't stop with the Toastmasters. He looked for frequent boosters to keep his attitude up. He propelled himself through countless biographies of some of history's greatest achievers for inspiration. He immersed himself in motivational tomes, such as those by Dale Carnegie. He picked the brains of those he met who were highly skilled in their fields. He gathered facts and figures on areas of interest and relentlessly pored over them until he'd absorbed them.

That pattern is one he's relied on ever since: Stay upbeat, study the experts, get all the facts from as many sources as possible, and you'll have an excellent model of how to conduct yourself—and your business.

O'Neil's biggest role models weren't all experts or well-known go-getters. The most influential ones were right at home.

Born in Oklahoma City, O'Neil was a year old when his parents divorced. He and his mother, Ann, moved to Muskogee, Okla., to share a house during the Depression with his maternal grandmother, Essie Jackson, his aunt, Lela, and an uncle. Ann worked as a clerk at J.C. Penney during the day to help support the family, so much of her son's care fell to his grandmother and aunt.

That pair encouraged O'Neil to work, and work hard. He did; his first job was selling magazines door to door in the third grade. As a youth, he also held paper and peanut-machine routes, clerked in grocery and drugstores, drove a bread truck, sold screen doors, manned a concession stand, worked in a lumberyard and parked cars for late-night boxing matches.

From each experience, O'Neil says, he gleaned bits of knowledge and even some wisdom.

"All those jobs were as important as school," he said.

He learned how to spot a market niche, for one. When selling screen doors while attending Southern Methodist University, O'Neil went to a new Texas subdivision one pleasant Saturday. Carrying the door, he made his pitch about added comfort and safety to families working in their yards. Soon curious neighbors wandered over to listen. In one afternoon, he sold 35 doors.

"It taught me timing was important because I went the day after a payday," he laughed. "And how important it is to demonstrate your product. You learn that through experience and work."

It wasn't just work that his grandmother and aunt pushed.

"My grandmother insisted that I go to church and Sunday school and learn the difference between right and wrong," O'Neil said. "She knew that I'd pretty much develop a conscience if I focused on that, and she was right."

He's steadfast about those values today. "There's always somebody who comes to you and says, 'We'll give you this if you give us a break here.' And I always say, 'No, that's not the right way to do things, we're not going to do that. We're going to do it the right way or not at all.'"

## At the Front

While his integrity remains firm, O'Neil is highly flexible when it comes to management structure. The traditional top-down management at most companies gets short shrift at DAI. "I've never believed you should have a strict structure where people are heading up their own little fiefdom," he said. "The business world is very complex, and you want to get as close to the front lines as you can."

His "maximum communication" model means that if O'Neil wants to talk to anyone in any of his companies, he does—and vice versa. O'Neil's office in his Los Angeles headquarters is purposely set in a high-traffic area easily accessible to employees.

"If he wants something done, Bill goes right to the person he knows can do it," said Cullen, who's known O'Neil for 38 years. "He once said to me that if he could, he'd put all his managers in a circle around him and all their people right around them. He wants access."

# APPENDIX

# How to Harness the Paper's Power in Five Steps

IBD has helped make a lot of millionaires. It's hard to quantify the exact number partly because it's a topic many people prefer to keep quiet about.

Nevertheless, countless interviews of successful IBD readers indicate that it takes at least three to six months or even longer to get all the rules down, follow them religiously, and use them the right way. Going through a few market cycles also helps.

If this sounds like too much work, then you might want to find a truly good mutual fund that has consistently beaten the S&P 500. Or you could search for a retail broker or hedge fund manager who truly understands how the market works and uses IBD's method consistently and successfully. But if you're willing to make an honest effort to learn how to make good stock picks without relying on tips and touts or the judgment of friends or family, read on.

Following the lead of O'Neil, who successfully incorporated his hard-won insights and strategies, will give you an unbiased guide to improving your investing skills. O'Neil has done the research, invested successfully, created the strategy you can follow, and built the tools to make it easier for others. His books can help take some of the stress out of investing by replacing guessing with a fact-based approach to finding the best stocks.

Consider the mastery of IBD-style investing as completing a five-step course at "The University of Wall Street." Or see it as a 5-kilometer run. Master one skill, and you've run 1 kilometer. Or, if your imagination will allow it, view the task as a sort of a modern pentathlon similar to the event held at the Athens Olympics in 2004. The key is to learn how to master five basic investing skills:

1. Understanding why only a few stocks in the market produce the biggest gains

2. Knowing the market's direction, and timing your entry to catch a big upward wave and to head into cash during a large downswing

3. Knowing how to choose and when to buy a good stock

4. Knowing when to sell a bad stock for minimal losses and when to sell a good stock for big gains

5. Staying positive and never giving up

I've taken the liberty of using the modern pentathlon as a framework. Here goes:

## First Event: Swimming

All serious swimmers are in great shape. Period. You can't cut corners in this sport. You have to learn the strokes, burn the body fat and put in the necessary laps in the pool. Stock investing is no different. It takes discipline, hard work, dedication and an eagerness to learn. There really are no secrets in the stock market. But you also need to shed common misconceptions on how the market really works. O'Neil's books shed light on what you need to know to do well. If investing were easy, no one would lose money, and everyone would personally know hundreds of people who had made it rich in the market.

*Training*

**1.** Read O'Neil's "How to Make Money in Stocks," Third Edition, from cover to cover. For those who have less time, read Chapters 1 to 13 (pages 3 to 164). You can learn in just several hours or a couple of days what O'Neil discovered during years and years of studying the market.

**2.** After reading the book, make a watch list of stocks by reading the following columns in IBD. Track their price-and-volume action. Watch how far they swing up and down. Note big increases or decreases in volume. In just a few weeks, you'll know the personality of a few stocks as if they were your best friends:

- "The Big Picture" and the "Market Pulse" (5 minutes per day)

- The "NYSE Real Most Active" column (5 minutes per day)

- The "Nasdaq Real Most Active" column (5 minutes per day)

- The "NYSE Stocks In The News" column (5 minutes per day)

- The "Nasdaq Stocks In The News" column (5 minutes per day)

- The "Investor's Corner" column (5 minutes per day)

**3.** Reread at least some parts of O'Neil's "How to Make Money" for further understanding. Like swimming, repetition is the key to mastery. Some readers tell us they mark up pages, and they read and reread the book, which helps them improve and invest more profitably.

**4.** Read features in *Internet & Technology, The New America, Health and Medicine, Industry Snapshot, and the IBD 100* to get a better grasp of the latest growth trends.

# Second Event: Riding

In this event, the athlete rides a horse and jumps over a series of 15 barriers on a 400-meter course. The human must guide the animal into the right rhythm. Timing is crucial. The successful IBD reader, or the human, must also understand the rhythm of the unique animal we call the "market." To do well, you must invest in stocks at the beginning of a new bull market cycle, **not** at the end of one. If the market is full of zip and scores of stocks are leaping to new highs on heavy volume, you must invest plenty of dollars in the best stocks to maximize those gains. But if the market is making only mild gains or moving sideways, you must not force trades and try too hard. As is true of the equestrian event, rushing into a precarious situation is costly. If market conditions stay choppy, it's better to sit back in cash and wait.

*Training*

**1.** After reading "The Big Picture" column, go to the "General Market & Sectors" page in IBD. Take a look at the notes about the price-and-volume action of the Nasdaq and S&P 500 indexes. On the same page, read the sidebar article highlighting the day's action. Draw a trend line that connects at least three intraday lows over a period of at least three months on the Nasdaq chart. Are you in an uptrend? A downtrend? A trendless market? Since roughly three out of four stocks follow the trend, you should invest actively only in strong markets. Always know that you can't push the market to do what you want it to do. Let the market tell you what is actually occurring—and then act accordingly.

**2.** Read Step 1, "Which Way Is the General Market Going?" in "The Successful Investor" by William O'Neil (pages 1 to 16). This gives an excellent course for new readers and veterans alike on major market tops and market bottoms from the early 1990s to today.

**3.** Watch for a follow-through (see the glossary for a definition of this key market phenomenon). Not all follow-throughs, which must come after a significant decline, do well. But IBD has found that every major bull market since 1900 had a follow-through. In the "Industry Groups" table, spot groups that are making big strides up the rankings. These groups tend to contain emerging new market stars.

**4.** If the market continues its strong uptrend, note which sectors are producing the largest number of stocks hitting 52-week highs. IBD makes this job easy. In the paper, all the stocks that have made new highs are grouped according to their broad industry sector. No other publication does this.

In a healthy market, the industry sectors with the largest number of stocks making 52-week highs tend to house the new leading stocks of the market. Also, check the "Groups With Highest % Of Stocks Making New Highs" table found at the end of the new lows list, also on the "Industry Groups" page. This small table also tracks new leaders.

**5.** Study the "Market Pulse" table, found within "The Big Picture" column, every day. Focus on the "Leading stocks up on volume" portion, and view their daily and weekly charts on investors.com. If you see a lot of stocks breaking out of solid bases and rapping new highs as the market surges on heavy volume, you're witnessing the earliest signal that a strong bull run is underway. That's the time to begin buying the best stocks. In this key phase of the market, a follow-through (when one or more of the major indexes gains at least 1.7% on heavier volume than the previous session) usually takes place on the 4th to 10th day of a new rally. Sometimes, it comes after 10 days. The important thing to remember is this: It can take as little as four days—yes, just four—for the market to turn!

## Third Event: Fencing

To win in this event, you have to know the precise moment to lunge and attack. Timing and strategy carry equal weight. So it is with buying a good stock. You can't simply buy a good stock at any time you feel like it. In a solid bull market, a stock is good only if it rises faster than its peers and breaks out of a well-crafted base to new highs. It remains a good stock if it hits more and more new highs. You can't buy a good stock at the bottom because you never know when bad news might pop up and lead to a collapse in price. The stock could go on and hit a new low, ripping apart your portfolio.

Let the stock prove its strength to you. Do not buy a stock until it surpasses its pivot point on huge volume. And never buy a stock if it's already more than 5% to 10% above the pivot. If a good stock has already vaulted 15%, 20% or more, let it go. IBD's golden rule is to sell a stock if it has fallen 7% to 8% below your purchase price. So if you buy it 15% or 20% above the proper buy point, you might get shaken out with a 7% or 8% loss. Why? A great stock often makes a normal, temporary price pullback before it resumes its rally. So have patience and keep looking. A truly strong market will offer new break-outs and new opportunities.

*Training*

**1.** Read the "Investor's Corner" column daily, and cut out articles that explain winning chart patterns, buy rules, proper handles, when to add shares to a winning position, how to hold a stock through its inevitable shakeouts, when to use margin and how to manage your portfolio. Make a notebook of these articles and review them regularly. Also read the "Winning Ways" chart analysis feature on Monday to get a feel of how the biggest winners from past bull markets acted at the start and end of their huge price runs. Some readers don't like to study old examples. They're only hurting themselves because it's not the stock itself that's important to know, it's the pattern of behavior. This pattern repeats itself over and over from bull market to bull market. Charts show the same human emotions at work in the market dynamic, year after year. Strong rallies reflect greed, weak rebounds illustrate hope, and fast sell-offs show fear.

**2.** Go to the IBD Learning Center at www.investors.com and go through the section "Lessons on Buying."

**3.** Read IBD's "Daily Stock Analysis" at www.investors.com (5 to 10 minutes/day). In this feature, markets writers pick apart the strong and weak elements of a stock that is forming a new base. The feature also points out sell signals in stocks that are falling fast.

**4.** Check the IBD "Screen of the Day," also on www.investors.com, which can help you form a watch list of potential winners. Even better, use the Daily Graphs Custom Screen Wizard to build additional watch lists.

## Fourth Event: Shooting

To do well in this event, you have to be cool under pressure. These Olympians try to pull the trigger in between heartbeats. Emotions have no place in this event. It is the same with selling stocks. When a stock turns against you and falls, you must become machinelike in your selling. Cut the loss at 7% or 8%. With experience and the use of charts, you can cut your losses even more quickly. O'Neil has said he's right on about half of his trades, and when he sees negative price-and-volume action, he'll cut losses quicker. So the average loss among his investment mistakes is around 5%.

*Training*

**1.** Go to the IBD Learning Center at www.investors.com, and then go through the section "Lessons on Selling."

**2.** Go over your past losing trades. Count how many stocks in which you lost more than 7% on the trade. Ask yourself: Why did I hold on to that stock? Understand what emotions you felt when the stock went down, be it denial or hope or a strong desire to prove the market wrong.

**3.** Study your winning stocks too. Ask yourself: Why did I sell? What was the proper sell signal provided by this chart? Write down the sell rule that triggered your action, and look at current holdings to see if the same sell rule can be applied elsewhere.

**4.** Read all the "Investor's Corner" columns that explain the 25-plus sell rules to help you lock in your hard-earned gains from good stocks. The IBD Archives on investors.com can aid your search. One series of Corner columns focusing on these sell rules ran from June 14, 2001, to July 23, 2001. Another series of 18 columns under the theme "Sell Rules in a Trading Market" ran from Jan. 8, 2003, to Feb. 3, 2003.

# Fifth Event: Cross-Country Running

Remember Mary Decker, the American hopeful who fell down during the 3,000-meter race at the 1984 Olympics in Los Angeles? Olympics fans remember photos of her face full of both anger and anguish as rival Zola Budd ran off without her. Falling down on the flat, smooth track happens rarely. But in cross-country running, falling down is par for the course. Runners can trip over a bulging tree root or rock. They lose their footing down a steep decline. To succeed in this event, if you fall, you have to get back up fast and keep moving.

Stock investing is also a race of perseverance. You will definitely take some hits. Losses are unavoidable in this game. But if you learn from your mistakes, you'll likely make fewer errors and improve your performance. Sometimes you'll pass up a zinger of a stock and gnash your teeth about it for weeks, maybe even months. Even when this happens, you have to keep going.

As O'Neil wrote on the final page of the first and second editions of "How to Make Money in Stocks," "My parting advice to you is: Have courage, be positive, and don't ever give up. Great opportunities occur every year in America. Get yourself prepared and go for it. You'll find that little acorns can grow into giant oaks. Anything is possible with persistence and hard work. It can be done, and your own determination to succeed is the most important element."

*Training*

**1.** Read 20-part series of "Investor's Corner" articles on investor psychology, from May 10, 2002, to June 7, 2002, available in the IBD Archives on www.investors.com. Another series of 24 articles on the same topic ran from March 29, 2004, to April 30, 2004.

**2.** Books by great traders can also provide perspective and inspiration. Some of the books recommended by O'Neil are "How I Made $2,000,000 in the Stock Market" by Nicolas Darvas, "Reminiscences of a Stock Operator" by Edwin Lefevre and "The Battle for Investment Survival" by Gerald Loeb.

**3.** Study your trades for the past 6 to 12 months, and separate them into winners and losers. Find the biggest percentage losers among your bad trades and print out their charts. Study the market's action at the time of your trade. Were you investing in a weak market? Had the stock already make a big run, and had it broken out of a late-stage base when you bought it?

**4.** Talk with someone who has done well with IBD, and learn from his or her experiences. Join an IBD Meetup in your area by visiting http://ibd.meetup.com. Or visit the IBD Forums, found on www.investors.com.

**5.** Finally, as O'Neil would always say: Don't give up!

# Glossary

**base**  A chart pattern in which a stock traces specific price-and-volume action before it begins a major rally to new highs and huge profits for those who got shares at the correct buy point. Studies by IBD founder William O'Neil and his research associates of the best-performing stocks from 1953 to 2003 show that these stocks typically form a base before launching the biggest phase of their price advance.

In a typical base, a stock makes a relatively mild decline in price or moves sideways for at least seven weeks (at least five weeks for a flat base) to as much as one year or more. Sound bases have a prior price uptrend of at least 30%. The most common base patterns are the *cup with handle, cup without a handle, double bottom, flat base, base on base,* and *saucer.*

For more information, visit the IBD Learning Center at www.investors.com and read "New Price Highs Mean New Opportunities" and "Chart Patterns Help You Spot The Right Time To Buy" in Course I. Also read pages 122 to 164 of "How to Make Money in Stocks," Third Edition, by William O'Neil.

**breakout**  The moment when a high-quality stock surges out of a base on increased and unusually heavy volume and surpasses the pivot point within a base. A strong breakout results in the stock's hitting new highs for a period of weeks or months, even years. For example, if a stock's pivot point is 33.10, the stock is breaking out when it rises to 33.10 and continues to go higher. (See *pivot point*.)

For more information, read pages 122 to 144 of "How to Make Money in Stocks," Third Edition, by William O'Neil. Also, read Lesson 9 (pages 43 to 49), "How to Buy at Just the Right Moment," in "24 Essential Lessons for Investment Success" by William O'Neil.

**CAN SLIM™**  The IBD acronym for the seven common characteristics all great performing stocks have before they make their biggest gains. You can significantly reduce your risk and increase returns by using the CAN SLIM™ Investment Research Tool as a fact-based performance checklist to evaluate a stock before you buy.

*C = current earnings per share*, which should be up 25% or more in the latest quarter versus the same period a year ago and in many cases accelerating in recent quarters. Quarterly sales should also be up 25% or more or accelerating over prior quarters.

*A = annual earnings*, which should be up 25% or more a year in each of the last three years. Annual return on equity (net income divided by average shareholders' equity over the past two years) should be 17% or more, or the annual pretax profit margin should be 17% or more.

*N = new product or service*. A company should have a new product or service that's innovative and fueling earnings growth. The stock should be emerging from a proper chart pattern and about to make a new high in price.

*S = supply and demand*. The number of shares outstanding can be large or small, but trading volume should be big at key points as the stock price increases.

*L = leader or laggard?* Buy the leading stock in a leading industry. A stock's Relative Price Strength Rating should be 80 or higher. Its IBD Composite Rating should preferably be 90 or higher.

*I = institutional sponsorship*, which should be increasing. Invest in stocks showing an increasing number of mutual fund owners in recent quarters and at least one or two of the better-performing growth-oriented mutual funds owning the stock. IBD's Accumulation/Distribution Rating gauges mutual fund activity in a stock.

*M = the market indexes.* The Dow, S&P 500 and Nasdaq should be in a confirmed uptrend since three out of four stocks follow the market's overall trend.

**chart**   A visual display of a stock's price-and-volume action. On investors.com, IBD provides two kinds of charts: (1) a daily chart, which shows a stock's intraday high, low and close and the share volume for each trading day; and (2) a weekly chart showing a weekly range of prices and the weekly close, as well as volume that week. For the days and weeks that a stock closes up in price, IBD charts paint both the price-range and volume bars in blue. Down days and down weeks and the corresponding volume bars are shown in red.

**Composite Rating**   An IBD SmartSelect Rating that combines all five IBD SmartSelect Ratings: EPS, RS, SMR, Industry Group RS, and Accumulation/Distribution. Of the five, EPS and RS get the most weight. The stock's price relative to its 52-week high is also factored in. Ratings range from 1 to 99, with 99 the best.

**cup-with-handle base**   A commonly seen chart pattern among the best growth stocks just before such a stock begins its huge price run. From a conceptual point of view, it is primarily a product of professional investor opinion and psychology plus the everyday forces of supply and demand among millions of investors.

Key criteria of a good cup-with-handle base are the following:

- At least seven weeks in length.

- A decline, frequently for five to seven weeks, that forms the left side of the cup and, in time, a rally off the low of the base to create the right side of the cup.

- Decline from the highest price in the base (simply known as "the high") to the lowest price (or "the bottom") running from 13% to 15% to as much as 40% during a bull market.

- Large or increasing spikes in volume as the stock builds the cup's right side.

- A downward-sloping handle (when measured along the lows of the price-range bars in the handle area). The handle forms in the upper half of the cup's overall price structure and must decline less in price in proportion to the decline in the base. Taken together, the price action from the initial decline to the handle resembles the silhouette of a teacup viewed from its side.

For more information and actual examples of cup-with-handle patterns, read pages 124 to 131 and 154 to 161 of "How to Make Money in Stocks," Third Edition, by William O'Neil. IBD subscribers can access the IBD Archives at www.investors.com and read past "Investor's Corner" columns explaining this important chart pattern, including "Many Top Stocks Emerge From A Cup-With-Handle Base" (June 4, 2004), "Some Cup Bases Last For Months, But Can Be Well Worth The Wait" (June 7, 2004), and the columns published on these dates in 2003: May 14, 15, 23; Oct. 7, 8; Nov. 7; and Dec. 2, 5, 15.

**Datagraph™** A unique graphic format designed by William O'Neil, founder of *Investor's Business Daily*, to collect and analyze stock-related data needed to discover the biggest winners in the stock market. Each stock Datagraph is 10 inches long and 7.5 inches wide and contains 126 key pieces of data, 98 of which are related to a company's fundamentals, and 28 are related to the stock's technical action. They include earnings per share, pretax margins and return on equity in each of the past nine years, earnings and revenue figures and year-over-year changes in the past 14 quarters, and the number of mutual funds that own the shares and total shares owned in the past 14 quarters. The Datagraphs are used by more than 400 of the top institutional investors around the world, including Merrill Lynch, J.P. Morgan, SwissRE, Wachovia Bank and the United Nations.

**distribution day**   The day when at least one of the major stock indexes (namely, the Nasdaq composite, S&P 500, and Dow) falls at least 0.5% on heavier trading volume than the previous session. The NYSE daily volume is monitored for changes in the S&P 500 and Dow. A series of three to five distribution days in just two to four weeks can signal the market is topping and that most stocks are likely headed for a decline. This is the time to consider selling some shares and keep watching for key sell signals by individual stocks.

For more information on distribution days, read pages 1 to 16 in "The Successful Investor" by William O'Neil and the "Big Picture" column in IBD on a daily basis.

**double-bottom base**   A key chart pattern that many of the greatest stocks carve before breaking out to new highs and huge price gains. On a daily or weekly chart, the stock's lows resemble a W shape. Examples of big winners producing the double-bottom base include American Power Conversion (1989–90), Sun Microsystems (1999), Apollo Group (2000) and eBay (2002).

Key criteria include the following:

- Two sell-offs, each over a few weeks' time, with the second sell-off usually undercutting the first low.

- A middle peak formed by an interim rebound in between the two sell-offs that fails to mark a new 52-week price high.

- A decline from the base's high to low of anywhere from 12% to as much as 30% during a bull market.

- The *pivot point*, or ideal buy point, is when the rally off the second bottom surpasses the peak of the interim rebound (or the middle part of the base) by at least 10 cents. In some cases, a handle forms after the stock makes a second low and then rallies back in price. Add 10 cents to the highest price within the handle to determine the pivot point, or ideal buy point.

For more information, read pages 132 to 133 and 162 to 163 of "How to Make Money in Stocks," Third Edition, by William O'Neil. Also, IBD subscribers can access "Investor's Corner" columns on the double-bottom base at IBD Archives on www.investors.com, including "Some Outstanding Stocks Form A Double Bottom In A Weak Market," (June 14, 2004), "After A Healthy Rally, Snack Firm Shot Out Of Double-Bottom Base" (Dec. 8, 2003) and "Cup, Saucer And Double-Bottom Patterns Often Reveal Symmetry" (Nov. 3, 2003).

**Earnings Per Share Rating (or EPS Rating)**   A proprietary IBD rating that compares a company's last two quarters and last 3 to 5 years of earnings per share growth and stability with that of all other public companies. Ratings range from 1 to 99, with 99 the best. A 95 rating means a company's earnings growth is superior to 95% of all stocks in the William O'Neil + Co. Database.

An IBD study of the 95 top performing small- and mid-cap stocks from 1994 to 1997 found that the median EPS Rating at the beginning of these stocks' big rallies was 79. In the same study, the median EPS Rating among 25 top performing large-cap stocks (market cap of roughly $4 billion and higher) was 80.

**flat base**   A chart pattern some great stocks form before breaking out and going on a run of new highs. The pattern must be a minimum of five weeks in length, and it does not fall more than 15% from the base's peak to trough. The stock's flat-looking sideways action indicates that institutional investors are not eager to sell shares. It often shows up when the major market indexes are struggling to move higher.

For examples of the flat base, read pages 133 to 134 in "How to Make Money in Stocks," Third Edition, by William O'Neil. Also, IBD subscribers can access "Investor's Corner" columns on the flat base at IBD Archives on www.investors.com, including "Flat-Base Patterns Can Lead To Exciting Stock Breakouts" (June 9, 2004) and "Flat Bases Help Solid Stocks Further Inflate Their Gains" (May 16, 2003).

**follow-through**   A confirmation that the general market has begun a potentially significant new uptrend. This uptrend can be seen specifically when at least one major index (namely, the Nasdaq composite, S&P 500, Dow) rises about 1.7% or more on heavier volume than the previous session, usually in the 4th to 10th day of a new rally attempt. Not all follow-throughs guarantee that a major new rally is taking place, but every major market bottom since 1900 has featured one.

For more information on follow-through days, read pages 1 to 16 in "The Successful Investor" by William O'Neil and the "Big Picture" column in IBD on a daily basis. Also, IBD subscribers can access "Investor's Corner" columns on the follow-through by going to IBD Archives at investors.com, including "Follow-Through On Oct. 15, 2002, Launched The Latest Bull Market" (Dec. 22, 2003) and "March 17 Follow-Through Launched A Fleet Of Breakouts" (Dec. 24, 2003).

**handle**    A period of stock action, generally between one week and up to six to eight weeks, that occurs toward the end of a cup, double-bottom or saucer pattern. In the handle, the stock trades in a tight price range near its 52-week high and drifts downward along the lows of its price-range bars on quiet volume.

A handle forms as nervous, disgruntled or uncommitted share-holders sell their shares and exit the stock. Those shares go into the hands of sturdier investors who are committed to holding the stock for the long term. The handle-forming process normally creates a shakeout of some weaker holders and clears the decks for a new rally by the stock. It also defines the correct buy point, or the pivot point. Add 10 cents to the highest price in the handle to get most pivot points.

For more information, read pages 124 to 129 of "How to Make Money in Stocks," Third Edition, by William O'Neil, as well as pages 45 to 49 in "24 Essential Lessons for Investment Success," also by William O'Neil. Also, IBD subscribers can access "Investor's Corner" columns on proper and improper handles at IBD Archives including "Handle Should Slant Downward" (Oct. 31, 2002), "Some Handles Feature Shakeouts" (Nov. 5, 2002), "Many Great Stocks Form A Handle Before Breaking Out" (March 19, 2003) and "Solid Handles Form In The Upper Half Of A Good Base" (March 21, 2003).

**pivot point**    The price a stock must go through in order to stage a sound breakout. When a stock goes through the pivot, it indicates an unusually high level of demand for shares by institutional and individual investors. This strong demand fuels a great stock's run to new highs and double- to triple-digit percentage gains as long as the stock base was formed in a sound and correct way. The stock's fundamentals (sales growth, earnings growth, return on equity and margins) must also be strong and among the best in the industry.

The pivot point for the base patterns are the following:

*cup with handle:* 10 cents above the highest price within the handle.

*cup without handle:* In general, 10 cents above the highest price on the cup's left side.

*double-bottom:* 10 cents above the middle peak. If the double-bottom base also has a handle, then the pivot is 10 cents above the handle's high.

*flat base:* 10 cents above the highest price in the base.

*saucer with handle:* 10 cents above the handle's high.

For more information, go through Course 1 in the IBD Learning Center at www.investors.com. Also read Chapter 12 in "How to Make Money in Stocks," Third Edition, by William O'Neil.

**Relative Price Strength Rating (or RS Rating)**  A proprietary IBD rating that compares a stock's price change in the past 12 months with all other stocks in the William O'Neil + Co. Database. Ratings range from 1 to 99, with 99 the best. A 95 RS Rating means a stock has outperformed 95% of all stocks over the past 12 months.

Generally, the strongest stocks in the market already have an RS Rating of at least 80 before they make the biggest part of their upward price moves. A study of the 95 top performing small- and mid-cap stocks from 1994 to 1997 found that the median RS Rating at the beginning of these stocks' big rallies was 84. In the same study, the median EPS Rating among 25 top performing large-cap stocks (market cap of roughly $4 billion and higher) was 73.

**Relative Strength line (or RS line)**  A line that plots a stock's price performance versus that of the S&P 500 large-cap index. When the line rises, the stock is outperforming the market. When it falls, the stock is underperforming. The RS line can be found on all daily and weekly charts in *Investor's Business Daily*'s "Daily Graphs Online" and investors.com. Studies of the biggest stock market winners from 1953 to 2001 show that the RS line climbs to new high ground before or at the same time a great stock breaks out of a solid base and vaults to new price highs.

**saucer base**   A chart pattern seen among some of the best stock market winners. It resembles the cup with handle, but it tends to be at least several months to over a year in length. The base's slow, steady decline and slow rise within the base resembles the silhouette of a saucer viewed from the side. Examples of stocks that formed saucer bases include Bank of America (BAC) from June 1994 to December 1995, Coca-Cola (KO) from June 1992 to March 1995 and Carbo Ceramics (CRR) from April 2002 to December 2003.

For more information on the saucer, read the "Investor's Corner" column "Saucer Base Wears Out Shareholders Before The Breakout" (June 11, 2004) and other columns on the saucer, available to IBD subscribers in the IBD Archives on www.investors.com.

**shakeout + 3**   A chart pattern seen among some of the best stock market winners, including Cisco Systems in October 1990. For a stock whose price is trading in the $20 to $30 range, a shakeout + 3 begins when it first falls to a low of, say, $22. After rebounding in price for a few weeks, the stock then suffers a second sell-off and undercuts the first low. If the market is in the early stages of a new rally, watch to see if the stock rebounds and rises $3 above the first low of $22 to reach $25. If volume is heavier than usual, the $25 level is the pivot point, or ideal buy point.

# INDEX

Seminars, IBD, 57, 88
"Shakeout + 3 points" chart pattern,
    36–37, 156
Sharpe, David, 89–90
Shaw, Craig, 56
Sherman, Kathy, xiv, 14, 15, 18–19, 21, 34,
    85, 122
Shuffle Master, 68
Silverthorne, Sean, 50
Sindona, Michele, xviii
Small Business Administration, 120
SmartLink, 51, 90, 97
Smith Barney, 16
SMR Rating, 96
Sohu.com, 68
Somoza, Anastasio, 103
Soviet Union, 103
S&P 500, 24, 36, 47, 66, 70, 137
*Sports Illustrated*, 86
Start-up costs, estimating, 85–87
State of Wisconsin Investment Board, 33
Stock ratings, 2
Stocks Highlighted in Yellow, 96
"Stocks in the News," 42
Subano, Jim, 70
*The Successful Investor* (William J.
    O'Neil), xii, 140
Sun Microsystems, 66
Sun Trust Banks, 33
Surgical Care Affiliates, 94–95
SwissRe, 33

**T**
Taylor, Frederick, 7
Technology stocks, 17
Television, 86–87
Temperato, Sam, 125
"10 Secrets of Success," 120–122, 124
Tennessee Consolidated Retirement Sys-
    tems, 33
Teva Pharmaceuticals, 94
Texas Instruments, 17, 48
Thorp, Bruce, 6
Timing the market, 60–61
Tjia, Monika, 56
Toastmasters, 134
Tracy, Brian, 93
Treasury bonds, 94
Treiser, Kinou, 123

**U**
United Airlines, 18–19
United Nations, 33
University of Texas, 71

Urban Outfitters, 32
U.S. Investing Championships, 19
*U.S. News & World Report*, 16
U.S. Treasury Bond Yield Curve Chart, 94
*USA Today*, x, xvi, 5, 7, 118–119
Usana Health, 68

**V**
Vartanian, Patricia, 69
Vatican, xvii–xviii
Vinciarelli, Patrizio, 120
Vitalink Communications Corp., 48
Von Alroth, Joanne, 123, 132

**W**
Warden, Chris, 127
*The Wall Street Journal*, xvi, 2, 3, 6–9,
    11–14, 16, 18–19, 24–26, 30, 34, 35,
    49, 89, 93
Wal-Mart, 30, 32, 73–74
Wang Labs, 17
Warner, H. M., 1
*Warren Buffet Speaks* (Janet Lowe), xv
*Washington Post*, xiv–xv, xvii
*Washington Times*, 15
Watergate, 9–10
Western Union, 1
William O'Neil + Co., Incorporated,
    xiii, xvii, 6, 11, 19, 31, 50, 88, 94,
    133
William O'Neil Direct Access, 33
Winans, R. Foster, 9
Wirthman, Lisa, 123
Wise, Christina, 55, 56
WONDA®, 33, 43
Wooden, John, 83
Woodward, Bob, 10
Woolman, Alex, 69
WorldCom, 66
Wright Brothers, 121

**X**
Xerox, 20

**Y**
Yahoo, 68, 87, 97
Yale University, 60
YMCA Retirement Fund, 33
Young & Rubicam, 24
"Your Portfolio" column, 100

**Z**
Zadeh, Norm, 19
Zenith Electronics, 48

# Acknowledgments

Dozens of people helped make this book a reality.

Many thanks to Chris Gessel, my main editor and mentor in the IBD newsroom, as well as to Kathleen Sherman, Bucky Fox, Karen Anderson, and Jessica Jensen for taking time out of their tight schedules to read the drafts, provide facts and give many valuable comments and suggestions.

Paul Lloyd-Strongin of IBD's art department generously spent many hours of his time to help me with photos, graphics and other art elements. Jovan Williams, Lora Findlay, Justin Nielsen, Piti Sirisutham, Scot Donaldson and Mary Ann Edwards also helped with pieces of art that also add color and pizzazz to the text.

I am indebted to Wes Mann, editor in chief at IBD, for his huge contribution to Chapter 4 of this book. That section really deserves Wes' byline.

Another round of thanks goes out to Terry Jones, Susan Warfel, Sally Doyle, Doug Rogers, Ralph Perrini, Deirdre Abbott, Sharon Brooks, Terri Chiodo, Harlan Ratzky, David Sharpe, Heather Davis, Eric Ruiz, Jonathan Hahn, Lisa Rubin, Margo Schuster, Jim Lucanish, Henry Godinez, Jewell Maddox, Jonah Keri, Craig Shaw, Nancy Gondo, Glenn Larkin, Jim Ellis, my wife Masako Saito and my sons Sean and Rick for their interviews, comments, support and assistance in so many ways during this project.

I'm grateful to Midori Sasaki, Yasuo Kurata, Yasuhiro Kishimoto, Hiroshi Sasaki, Bill May, Antonio Kamiya, Shiro Yoneyama, Hisa Miyatake and other editors and friends during my days as a bamboo-green reporter at the Kyodo global news agency in Tokyo, Japan. Thanks to the great English teachers at Shawnee Middle and High School in Lima, Ohio, particularly Cecily Crider, Mrs. Witter, Marie Stevens and Marge Bush, who sparked in me an interest in writing that will last a lifetime.

I appreciate the warm support and expertise from Philip Ruppel, Mary Glenn, Lynda Luppino, Ruth Mannino, Marci Nugent, and the rest of the staff at McGraw-Hill Trade. Finally, to Bill O'Neil, thank you for your constant search for truth, energy, wisdom, and determination. It's infectious.

# INVESTOR'S BUSINESS DAILY®

*introduces*

# PREMIUM SERVICES

## at investors.com

## Get *unprecedented* access to 8,000 stocks!

## Daily Graphs Online®

Access technical, fundamental and proprietary data for 8,000 companies tracked in the Database*. Features include:

* Premium daily, weekly and intraday stock graphs
* Proprietary ratings, quarterly and annual earnings and sales data
* Graphs of market indices and market indicators
* Valuable reports of stocks meeting special criteria
* Detailed technical and fundamental data & more!

## Custom Screen Wizard

Search the entire Database* for stocks that match your own specific criteria using up to 70 data items in eight categories:

1) IBD *SmartSelect*® Ratings
2) Earnings
3) Sales
4) Industry & Sector
5) Shares & Holdings
6) Price & Volume
7) Margins & Ratios
8) General

## Industry Groups

Track the intraday performance of the 197 Industry Groups** and easily identify leading stocks in leading industry groups. Includes:

* Complete lists of all stocks in the 197 Industry Groups**
* Best and worst groups based on intraday performance and 6-month price performance
* Ten industry groups with the most stocks trading at new 52-week highs and new 52-week lows